Letters of Edward

Fanny Kemble

(1871-1883)

Edward FitzGerald

Editor: William Aldis Wright

Alpha Editions

This edition published in 2022

ISBN : 9789356718197

Design and Setting By
Alpha Editions
www.alphaedis.com
Email - info@alphaedis.com

LETTERS OF EDWARD FITZGERALD TO FANNY KEMBLE
1871-1883

'Letters . . . such as are written from wise men, are, of all the words of man, in my judgment the best.'—BACON.

The following letters, addressed by Edward FitzGerald to his life-long friend Fanny Kemble, form an almost continuous series, from the middle of 1871 to within three weeks of his death in 1883. They are printed as nearly as possible as he wrote them, preserving his peculiarities of punctuation and his use of capital letters, although in this he is not always consistent. In writing to me in 1873 he said, 'I love the old Capitals for Nouns.' It has been a task of some difficulty to arrange the letters in their proper order, in consequence of many of them being either not dated at all or only imperfectly dated; but I hope I have succeeded in giving them, approximately at least, in their true sequence. The notes which are added are mainly for the purpose of explaining allusions, and among them will be found extracts from other letters in my possession which have not been published. The references to the printed 'Letters' are to the separate edition in the Eversley Series, 2 vols. (Macmillans, 1894).

In a letter to Mr. Arthur Malkin, October 15, 1854 ('Further Records,' ii. 193), Mrs. Kemble enunciates her laws of correspondence, to which frequent reference is made in the present series as the laws of the Medes and Persians: 'You bid me not answer your letter, but I have certain *organic laws* of correspondence from which nothing short of a miracle causes me to depart; as, for instance, I never write till I am written to, I always write when I am written to, and I make a point of always returning the same amount of paper I receive, as you may convince yourself by observing that I send you two sheets of note-paper and Mary Anne only half one, though I have nothing more to say to you, and I have to her.'

WILLIAM ALDIS WRIGHT.

January 1895.

I.

DEAR MRS. KEMBLE,

I asked Donne to tell you, if he found opportunity, that some two months ago I wrote you a letter, but found it so empty and dull that I would not send it to extort the Reply which you feel bound to give. I should have written to tell you so myself; but I heard from Donne of the Wedding soon about to be, and I would not intrude then. Now that is over [3a]—I hope to the satisfaction of you all—and I will say my little say, and you will have to Reply, according to your own Law of Mede and Persian.

It is a shame that one should only have oneself to talk about; and yet that is all I have; so it shall be short. If you will but tell me of yourself, who have read, and seen, and done, so much more, you will find much more matter for your pen, and also for my entertainment.

Well, I have sold my dear little Ship, [3b] because I could not employ my Eyes with reading in her Cabin, where I had nothing else to do. I think those Eyes began to get better directly I had written to agree to the Man's proposal. Anyhow, the thing is done; and so now I betake myself to a Boat, whether on this River here, or on the Sea at the Mouth of it.

Books you see I have nothing to say about. The Boy who came to read to me made such blundering Work that I was forced to confine him to a Newspaper, where his Blunders were often as entertaining as the Text which he mistook. We had 'hangarues' in the French Assembly, and, on one occasion, 'ironclad Laughter from the Extreme Left.' Once again, at the conclusion of the London news, 'Consolations closed at 91, ex Div.'—And so on. You know how illiterate People will jump at a Word they don't know, and twist it in[to] some word they are familiar with. I was telling some of these Blunders to a very quiet Clergyman here some while ago, and he assured me that a poor Woman, reading the Bible to his Mother, read off glibly, 'Stand at a Gate and swallow a Candle.' I believe this was no Joke of his: whether it were or not, here you have it for what you may think it worth.

I should be glad to hear that you think Donne looking and seeming well. Archdeacon Groome, who saw him lately, thought he looked very jaded: which I could not wonder at. Donne, however, writes as if in good Spirits—brave Man as he is—and I hope you will be able to tell me that he is not so much amiss. He said that he was to be at the Wedding.

You will tell me too how long you remain in England; I fancy, till Winter: and then you will go to Rome again, with its new Dynasty installed in it. I fancy I should not like that so well as the old; but I suppose it's better for the Country.

I see my Namesake (Percy) Fitzgerald advertizes a Book about the Kembles. That I shall manage to get sight of. He made far too long work of Garrick. I should have thought the Booksellers did not find that pay, judging by the price to which Garrick soon came down. Half of it would have been enough.

Now I am going for a Sail on the famous River Deben, to pass by the same fields of green Wheat, Barley, Rye, and Beet-root, and come back to the same Dinner. Positively the only new thing we have in Woodbridge is a Waxen Bust (Lady, of course) at the little Hairdresser's opposite. She turns slowly round, to our wonder and delight; and I caught the little Barber the other day in the very Act of winding her up to run her daily Stage of Duty. Well; she has not got to answer Letters, as poor Mrs. Kemble must do to hers always sincerely

E. F.G.

II.

WOODBRIDGE. NOV[r]. 2/71.

DEAR MRS. KEMBLE,

Is it better not to write at all than only write to plead that one has nothing to say? Yet I don't like to let the year get so close to an end without reminding you of me, to whom you have been always so good in the matter of replying to my letters, as in other ways.

If I can tell you nothing of myself: no Books read because of no Eyes to read them: no travel from home because of my little Ship being vanished: no friends seen, except Donne, who came here with Valentia for two days—*you* can fill a sheet like this, I know, with some account of yourself and your Doings: and I shall be very glad to hear that all is well with you. Donne said he believed you were in Ireland when he was here; and he spoke of your being very well when he had last seen you; also telling me he thought you were to stay in England this winter. By the by, I also heard of Mrs. Wister being at Cambridge; not Donne told me this, but Mr. Wright, the Bursar of Trinity: and every one who speaks of her says she is a very delightful Lady. Donne himself seemed very well, and in very good Spirits, in spite of all his domestic troubles. What Courage, and Good Temper, and Self-sacrifice! Valentia (whom I had not seen these dozen years) seemed a very sensible, unaffected Woman.

I would almost bet that you have not read my Namesake's Life of your Namesakes, which I must borrow another pair of Eyes for one day. My Boy-reader gave me a little taste of it from the Athenæum; as also of Mr. Harness' Memoirs, [6] which I must get at.

This is a sorry sight [7] of a Letter:—do not trouble yourself to write a better—that you must, in spite of yourself—but write to me a little about yourself; which is a matter of great Interest to yours always

E. F.G.

III.

[*Nov.* 1871.]

DEAR MRS. KEMBLE,

I ought to be much obliged to you for answering my last letter with an uneasy hand, as you did. So I do thank you: and really wish that you would not reply to this under any such pain: but how do I know but that very pain will make you more determined to reply? I must only beg you not to do so: and thus wash *my* hands of any responsibilities in the matter.

And what will you say when I tell you that I can hardly pity one who suffers from Gout; though I would undoubtedly prefer that you should be free from that, or any other ailment. But I have always heard that Gout exempts one from many other miseries which Flesh is heir to: at any rate, it almost always leaves the Head clear: and that is so much! My Mother, who suffered a good deal, used often to say how she was kept awake of nights by the Pain in her feet, or hands, but felt so clear aloft that she made Night pass even agreeably away with her reflections and recollections.

And you have your recollections and Reflections which you are gathering into Shape, you say, in a Memoir of your own Life. And you are good enough to say that you would read it to me if I—were good enough to invite you to my House here some Summer Day! I doubt that Donne has given you too flattering an account of my house, and me: you know he is pleased with every one and everything: I know it also, and therefore no longer dissuade him from spending his time and money in a flying Visit here in the course of his Visits to other East Anglian friends and Kinsmen. But I feel a little all the while as if I were taking all, and giving nothing in return: I mean, about Books, People, etc., with which a dozen years discontinuance of Society, and, latterly, incompetent Eyes, have left me in the lurch. If you indeed will come and read your Memoir to me, I shall be entitled to be a Listener only: and you shall have my Château all to yourself for as long as you please: only do not expect me to be quite what Donne may represent.

It is disgusting to talk so much about oneself: but I really think it is better to say so much on this occasion. If you consider my circumstances, you will perhaps see that I am not talking unreasonably: I am sure, not with sham humility: and that I am yours always and sincerely

E. F.G.

P.S. I should not myself have written so soon again, but to apprise you of a brace of Pheasants I have sent you. Pray do not write expressly to acknowledge them:—only tell me if they don't come. I know you thank me. [9]

IV.

[27 *Feb.*, 1872.]

DEAR MRS. KEMBLE,

Had I anything pleasant to write to you, or better Eyes to write it with, you would have heard from me before this. An old Story, by way of Apology— to one who wants no such Apology, too. Therefore, true though it be there is enough of it.

I hear from Mowbray Donne that you were at his Father's Lectures, [10a] and looking yourself. So that is all right. Are your Daughters—or one of them—still with you? I do not think you have been to see the Thanksgiving Procession, [10b] for which our Bells are even now ringing— the old Peal which I have known these—sixty years almost—though at that time it reached my Eyes (*sic*) through a Nursery window about two miles off. From that window I remember seeing my Father with another Squire [10c] passing over the Lawn with their little pack of Harriers—an almost obliterated Slide of the old Magic Lantern. My Mother used to come up sometimes, and we Children were not much comforted. She was a remarkable woman, as you said in a former letter: and as I constantly believe in outward Beauty as an Index of a Beautiful Soul within, I used sometimes to wonder what feature in her fine face betrayed what was not so good in her Character. I think (as usual) the Lips: there was a twist of Mischief about them now and then, like that in—the Tail of a Cat!— otherwise so smooth and amiable. I think she admired your Mother as much as any one she knew, or had known.

And (I see by the Athenæum) Mr. Chorley is dead, [11] whom I used to see at your Father's and Sister's houses. Born in 1808 they say: so, one year older than yours truly E. F.G.—who, however, is going to live through another page of Letter-paper. I think he was a capital Musical Critic, though he condemned Piccolomini, who was the last Singer I heard of Genius, Passion, and a Voice that told both. I am told she was no Singer: but that went some way to make amends. Chorley, too, though an irritable, nervous creature, as his outside expressed, was kind and affectionate to Family and Friend, I always heard. But I think the Angels must take care to keep in tune when he gets among them.

This is a wretched piece of Letter to extort the Answer which you feel bound to give. But I somehow wished to write: and not to write about myself; and so have only left room to say—to repeat—that I am yours ever sincerely

E. F.G.

V.

[1872.]

DEAR MRS. KEMBLE,

I set off with a Letter to you, though I do not very well know how I am to go on with it. But my Reader has been so disturbed by a Mouse in the room that I have dismissed him—9½ p.m.—and he has been reading (so far as he could get on) Hawthorne's Notes of Italian Travel: which interest me very much indeed, as being the Notes of a Man of Genius who will think for himself independently of Murray &c. And then his Account of Rome has made me think of you more than once. We have indeed left off to-night at Radicofani: but, as my Boy is frightened away by the Mouse, I fancy I will write to you before I take my one Pipe—which were better left alone, considering that it gives but half an hour's rather pleasant musing at the expense of a troubled night. Is it not more foolish then to persist in doing this than being frightened at a Mouse? This is not a mere fancy of the Boy—who is not a Fool, nor a 'Betty,' and is seventeen years old: he inherits his terror from his Mother, he says: positively he has been in a cold Sweat because of this poor little thing in the room: and yet he is the son of a Butcher here. So I sent him home, and write to you instead of hearing him read Hawthorne. He is to bring some poisoned Wheat for the Mouse to-morrow.

Another Book he read me also made me think of you: Harness: whom I remember to have seen once or twice at your Father's years ago. The Memoir of him (which is a poor thing) still makes one like—nay, love— him—as a kindly, intelligent, man. I think his latter letters very pleasant indeed.

I do not know if you are in London or in your 'Villeggiatura' [13a] in Kent. Donne must decide that for me. Even my Garden and Fields and Shrubs are more flourishing than I have yet seen them at this time of Year: and with you all is in fuller bloom, whether you be in Kent or Middlesex. Are you going on with your Memoir? Pray read Hawthorne. I dare say you do not quite forget Shakespeare now and then: dear old Harness, reading him to the last!

Pray do you read Annie Thackeray's new Story [13b] in Cornhill? She wrote me that she had taken great pains with it, and so thought it might not be so good as what she took less pains with. I doated on her Village on the Cliff, but did not care for what I had read of hers since: and this new Story I have not seen! And pray do you doat on George Eliot?

Here are a few questions suggested for you to answer—as answer I know you will. It is almost a Shame to put you to it by such a piece of inanity as this letter. But it is written: it is 10 p.m. A Pipe—and then to Bed—with what Appetite for Sleep one may.

And I am yours sincerely always

E. F.G.

VI.

WOODBRIDGE: *June* 6, [1872].

DEAR MRS. KEMBLE,

Some little while ago I saw in a London Book Catalogue 'Smiles and Tears—a Comedy by Mrs. C. Kemble'—I had a curiosity to see this: and so bought it. Do you know it?—Would you like to have it? It seems to be ingeniously contrived, and of easy and natural Dialogue: of the half sentimental kind of Comedy, as Comedies then were (1815) with a serious—very serious—element in it—taken from your Mother's Friend's, Mrs. Opie's (what a sentence!) story of 'Father and Daughter'—the seduced Daughter, who finds her distracted Father writing her name on a Coffin he has drawn on the Wall of his Cell—All ends happily in the Play, however, whatever may be the upshot of the Novel. But an odd thing is, that this poor Girl's name is 'Fitz Harding'—and the Character was played by Miss Foote: whether before, or after, her seduction by Colonel Berkeley I know not. The Father was played by Young.

Sir Frederick Pollock has been to see me here for two days, [15] and put me up to much that was going on in the civilized World. He was very agreeable indeed: and I believe his Visit did him good. What are you going to do with your Summer? Surely never came Summer with more Verdure:

and I somehow think we shall have more rain to keep the Verdure up, than for the last few years we have had.

I am quite sure of the merit of George Eliot, and (I should have thought) of a kind that would suit me. But I have not as yet found an Appetite for her. I have begun taking the Cornhill that I may read Annie Thackeray—but I have not found Appetite for her as yet. Is it that one recoils from making so many new Acquaintances in Novels, and retreats upon one's Old Friends, in Shakespeare, Cervantes, and Sir Walter? Oh, I read the last as you have lately been reading—the Scotch Novels, I mean: I believe I should not care for the Ivanhoes, Kenilworths, etc., any more. But Jeanie Deans, the Antiquary, etc., I shall be theirs as long as I am yours sincerely

E. F.G.

VII.

WOODBRIDGE: *August* 9, [1872].

DEAR MRS. KEMBLE,

I think I shall hear from you once again before you go abroad. To Rome! My Brother Peter also is going to winter there: but you would not have much in common with him, I think, so I say nothing of an Acquaintance between you.

I have been having Frederick Tennyson with me down here. [16a] He has come to England (from Jersey where his home now is) partly on Business, and partly to bring over a deaf old Gentleman who has discovered the Original Mystery of Free-masonry, by means of Spiritualism. The Freemasons have for Ages been ignorant, it seems, of the very Secret which all their Emblems and Signs refer to: and the question is, if they care enough for their own Mystery to buy it of this ancient Gentleman. If they do not, he will shame them by Publishing it to all the world. Frederick Tennyson, who has long been a Swedenborgian, a Spiritualist, and is now even himself a Medium, is quite grand and sincere in this as in all else: with the Faith of a Gigantic Child—pathetic and yet humorous to consider and consort with.

I went to Sydenham for two days to visit the Brother I began telling you of: and, at a hasty visit to the Royal Academy, caught a glimpse of Annie Thackeray: [16b] who had first caught a glimpse of me, and ran away from her Party to seize the hands of her Father's old friend. I did not know her at first: was half overset by her cordial welcome when she told me who she was; and made a blundering business of it altogether. So much so, that I could not but write afterwards to apologize to her: and she returned as kind an Answer as she had given a Greeting: telling me that my chance Apparition had been to her as 'A message from Papa.' It was really something to have been of so much importance.

I keep intending to go out somewhere—if for no other reason than that my rooms here may be cleaned! which they will have it should be done once a year. Perhaps I may have to go to my old Field of Naseby, where Carlyle wants me to erect a Stone over the spot where I dug up some remains of those who were slain there over two hundred years ago, for the purpose of satisfying him in his Cromwell History. This has been a fixed purpose of his these twenty years: I thought it had dropped from his head: but it cropped up again this Spring, and I do not like to neglect such wishes. Ever yours

E. F.G.

VIII.

April 22, [1873.]

DEAR MRS. KEMBLE,

One last word about what you call my 'Half-invitation' to Woodbridge. In one sense it is so; but not in the sense you imagine.

I never do invite any of my oldest Friends to come and see me, am almost distressed at their proposing to do so. If they take me in their way to, or from, elsewhere (as Donne in his Norfolk Circuit) it is another matter.

But I have built a pleasant house just outside the Town, where I never live myself, but keep it mainly for some Nieces who come there for two or three months in the Summer: and, when they are not there, for any Friends who like to come, for the Benefit of fresh Air and Verdure, *plus* the company of their Host. An Artist and his Wife have stayed there for some weeks for the last two years; and Donne and Valentia were to have come, but that they went abroad instead.

And so, while I should even deprecate a Lady like you coming thus far only for my sake, who ought rather to go and ask Admission at your Door, I should be glad if you liked to come to my house for the double purpose aforesaid.

My Nieces have hitherto come to me from July to September or October. Since I wrote to you, they have proposed to come on May 21; though it may be somewhat later, as suits the health of the Invalid—who lives on small means with her elder Sister, who is her Guardian Angel. I am sure that no friend of mine—and least of all you—would dissent from my making them my first consideration. I never ask them in Winter, when I think they are better in a Town: which Town has, since their Father's

Death, been Lowestoft, where I see them from time to time. Their other six sisters (one only married) live elsewhere: all loving one another, notwithstanding.

Well: I have told you all I meant by my 'Half-Invitation.' These N.E. winds are less inviting than I to these parts; but I and my House would be very glad to entertain you to our best up to the End of May, if you really liked to see Woodbridge as well as yours always truly

E. F. G.

P.S.—You tell me that, once returned to America, you think you will not return ever again to England. But you will—if only to revisit those at Kenilworth—yes, and the blind Lady you are soon going to see in Ireland [19a]—and two or three more in England beside—yes, and old England itself, 'with all her faults.'

By the by:—Some while ago [19b] Carlyle sent me a Letter from an American gentleman named Norton (once of the N. American Review, C. says, and a most amiable, intelligent Gentleman)—whose Letter enclosed one from Ruskin, which had been entrusted to another American Gentleman named Burne Jones—who kept it in a Desk ten years, and at last forwarded it as aforesaid—to me! The Note (of Ruskin's) is about one of the Persian Translations: almost childish, as that Man of Genius is apt to be in his Likes as well as Dislikes. I dare say he has forgotten all about Translator and Original long before this. I wrote to thank Mr. Norton for

(*Letter unfinished.*)

IX.

[1873.]

DEAR MRS. KEMBLE,

It is scarce fair to assail you on your return to England with another Letter so close on that to which you have only just answered—you who *will* answer! I wish you would consider this Letter of mine an Answer (as it really is) to that last of yours; and before long I will write again and call on you then for a Reply.

What inspires me now is, that, about the time you were writing to me about Burns and Béranger, I was thinking of them 'which was the Greater Genius?'—I can't say; but, with all my Admiration for about a Score of the Frenchman's almost perfect Songs, I would give all of them up for a Score of Burns' Couplets, Stanzas, or single Lines scattered among those quite *im*perfect Lyrics of his. Béranger, no doubt, was The *Artist*; which still is not the highest Genius—witness Shakespeare, Dante, Æschylus, Calderon, to the contrary. Burns assuredly had more *Passion* than the Frenchman; which is not Genius either, but a great Part of the Lyric Poet still. What Béranger might have been, if born and bred among Banks, Braes, and Mountains, I cannot tell: Burns had that advantage over him. And then the Highland Mary to love, amid the heather, as compared to Lise the Grisette in a Parisian Suburb! Some of the old French Virelays and *Vaux-de-vire* come much nearer the Wild Notes of Burns, and go to one's heart like his; Béranger never gets so far as that, I think. One knows he will come round to his pretty *refrain* with perfect grace; if he were more Inspired he couldn't.

> 'My Love is like the red, red, Rose
>   That's newly sprung in June,
> My Love is like the Melody
>   That's sweetly play'd in tune.'

and he will love his Love,

> 'Till a' the Seas gang Dry'

Yes—Till a' the Seas gang dry, my Dear. And then comes some weaker stuff about Rocks melting in the Sun. All Imperfect; but that red, red Rose has burned itself into one's silly Soul in spite of all. Do you know that one of Burns' few almost perfect stanzas was perfect till he added two Syllables to each alternate Line to fit it to the lovely Music which almost excuses such a dilution of the Verse?

> 'Ye Banks and Braes o' bonnie Doon,
>   How can ye bloom (so fresh) so fair?
> Ye little Birds how can ye sing,
>   And I so (weary) full of care!
> Thou'lt break my heart, thou little Bird,
>   That sings (singest so) upon the Thorn:
> Thou minds me of departed days
>   That never shall return
>   (Departed never to) return.'

Now I shall tell you two things which my last Quotation has recalled to me.

Some thirty years ago A. Tennyson went over Burns' Ground in Dumfries. When he was one day by Doon-side—'I can't tell how it was, Fitz, but I fell into a Passion of Tears'—And A. T. not given to the melting mood at all.

No. 2. My friend old Childs of the romantic town of Bungay (if you can believe in it!) told me that one day he started outside the Coach in company with a poor Woman who had just lost Husband or Child. She talked of her Loss and Sorrow with some Resignation; till the Coach happened to pull up by a roadside Inn. A 'little Bird' was singing somewhere; the poor Woman then broke into Tears, and said—'I could bear anything but that.' I dare say she had never even heard of Burns: but he had heard the little Bird that he knew would go to all Hearts in Sorrow.

Béranger's Morals are Virtue as compared to what have followed him in France. Yet I am afraid he partly led the way. Burns' very *Passion* half excused him; so far from its being Refinement which Burke thought deprived Vice of half its Mischief!

Here is a Sermon for you, you see, which you did not compound for: nor I neither when I began my Letter. But I think I have told you the two Stories aforesaid which will almost deprive my sermon of half its Dulness. And I am now going to transcribe you a *Vau-de-vire* of old Olivier de Basselin, [23a] which will show you something of that which I miss in Béranger. But I think I had better write it on a separate Paper. Till which, what think you of these lines of Clément Marot on the Death of some French Princess who desired to be buried among the Poor? [23b]

[P.S.—These also must go on the Fly-leaf: being too long, Alexandrine, for these Pages.]

What a Letter! But if you are still at your Vicarage, you can read it in the Intervals of Church. I was surprised at your coming so early from Italy: the famous Holy Week there is now, I suppose, somewhat shorn of its Glory.—If you were not so sincere I should think you were persiflaging me about the Photo, as applied to myself, and yourself. Some years ago I said—and now say—I wanted one of you; and if this letter were not so long, would tell you a little how to sit. Which you would not attend to; but I should be all the same, your long-winded

Friend
E. F.G.

X.

WOODBRIDGE, *May* 1, [1873.]

DEAR MRS. KEMBLE,

I am very glad that you will be Photographed: though not by the Ipswich Man who did me, there are no doubt many much better in London.

Of course the whole Figure is best, if it can be artistically arranged. But certainly the safe plan is to venture as little as possible when an Artist's hand cannot harmonize the Lines and the Lights, as in a Picture. And as the Face is the Chief Object, I say the safest thing is to sit for the Face, neck, and Shoulders only. By this, one not only avoids any conflict about Arms and Hands (which generally disturb the Photo), but also the Lines and Lights of Chair, Table, etc.

For the same reason, I vote for nothing but a plain Background, like a Curtain, or sober-coloured Wall.

I think also that there should be no White in the Dress, which is apt to be too positive for the Face. Nothing nearer White than such material as (I think) Brussels Lace (?) of a yellowish or even dirty hue; of which there may be a Fringe between Dress and Skin. I have advised Men Friends to sit in a—dirty Shirt!

I think a three-quarter face is better that a Full; for one reason, that I think the Sitter feels more at ease looking somewhat away, rather than direct at the luminous Machine. This will suit you, who have a finely turned Head, which is finely placed on Neck and Shoulders. But, as your Eyes are fine also, don't let them be turned too much aside, nor at all downcast: but simply looking as to a Door or Window a little on one side.

Lastly (!) I advise sitting in a lightly clouded Day; not in a bright Sunlight at all.

You will think that I am preaching my own Photo to you. And it is true that, though I did not sit with any one of these rules in my head; but just as I got out of a Cab, etc., yet the success of the Thing made me consider afterward why it succeeded; and I have now read you my Lecture on the Subject. Pray do not forgo your Intention—nay, your Promise, as I regard it—to sit, and send me the result. [25]

Here has been a bevy of Letters, and long ones, from me, you see. I don't know if it is reasonable that one should feel it so much easier to write to a Friend in England than to the same Friend abroad; but so it is, with me at least. I suppose that a Letter directed to Stoneleigh will find you before you leave—for America!—and even after that. But I shall not feel the same confidence and ease in transcribing for you pretty Norman Songs, or gossiping about them as I have done when my Letters were only to travel to Kenilworth: which very place—which very name of a Place—makes the English world akin. I suppose you have been at Stratford before this—an event in one's Life. It was not the Town itself—or even the Church—that touched me most: but the old Footpaths over the Fields which He must have crossed three Centuries ago.

Spedding tells me he is nearing Land with his Bacon. And one begins to think Macready a Great Man amid the Dwarfs that now occupy his Place.

Ever yours sincerely

E. F.G.

September 18/73.

DEAR MRS. KEMBLE,

I have not forgotten you at all, all these months—What a Consolation to you! But I felt I had nothing to send among the Alps after you: I have been nowhere but for two Days to the Field of Naseby in Northamptonshire, where I went to identify the spot where I dug up the Dead for Carlyle thirty years ago. I went; saw; made sure; and now—the Trustees of the Estate won't let us put up the Memorial stone we proposed to put up; they approve (we hear) neither of the Stone, nor the Inscription; both as plain and innocent as a Milestone, says Carlyle, and indeed much of the same Nature. This Decision of the foolish Trustees I only had some ten days ago: posted it to Carlyle who answered from Dumfries; and his Answer shows that he is in full vigour, though (as ever since I have known him) he protests that Travelling has utterly discomfited him, and he will move no more. But it is very silly of these Trustees. [28a]

And, as I have been nowhere, I have seen no one; nor read anything but the Tichborne Trial, and some of my old Books—among them Walpole, Wesley, and Johnson (Boswell, I mean), three very different men whose Lives extend over the same times, and whose diverse ways of looking at the world they lived in make a curious study. I wish some one would write a good Paper on this subject; I don't mean to hint that I am the man; on the contrary, I couldn't at all; but I could supply some [one] else with some material that he would not care to hunt up in the Books perhaps.

Well: all this being all, I had no heart to write—to the Alps! And now I remember well you told me you [were] coming back to England—for a little while—a little while—and then to the New World for ever—which I don't believe! [28b] Oh no! you will come back in spite of yourself, depend upon it—and yet I doubt that my saying so will be one little reason why you will not! But do let me hear of you first: and believe me ever yours

E. F.G.

XII.

[WOODBRIDGE, 1873.]

DEAR MRS. KEMBLE,

You must attribute this third Letter to an '*Idée*' that has come into my head relating to those Memoirs of yourself which you say you are at some loss to dispose of. I can easily understand that your Children, born and bred (I think) in another World, would not take so much interest in them as some of your old Friends who make part of your Recollections: as you yourself occupy much of theirs. But then they are *old* Friends; and are not their Children, Executors and Assigns, as little to be depended on as your own Kith and Kin? Well; I bethink me of one of your old Friends' Children whom I could reckon upon for you, as I would for myself: Mowbray Donne: the Son of one who you know loves you of old, and inheriting all his Father's Loyalty to his Father's Friends. I am quite convinced that he is to be perfectly depended upon in all respects for this purpose; for his Love, his Honour, and his Intelligence. I should then make him one day read the Memoirs to me—for I can't be assured of my own Eyes interpreting your MS. without so much difficulty as would disturb one's Enjoyment, or Appreciation, of such a Memoir. Unless indeed you should one day come down yourself to my Château in dull Woodbridge, and there read it over, and talk it over.

Well; this is what I seriously advise, always supposing that you have decided not to print and publish the Memoir during your Life. No doubt you could make money of it, beside 'bolting up' [30] such Accident as the Future comprehends. The latter would, I know, be the only recommendation to you.

I don't think you will do at all as I advise you. But I nevertheless advise you as I should myself in case I had such a Record as you have to leave behind me.—

Now once more for French Songs. When I was in Paris in 1830, just before that Revolution, I stopped one Evening on the Boulevards by the Madeleine to listen to a Man who was singing to his Barrel-organ. Several passing 'Blouses' had stopped also: not only to listen, but to join in the Songs, having bought little '*Libretti*' of the words from the Musician. I bought one too; for, I suppose, the smallest French Coin; and assisted in the Song which the Man called out beforehand (as they do Hymns at Church), and of which I enclose you the poor little Copy. '*Le Bon Pasteur*, s'il vous plait'—I suppose the Circumstances: the 'beau temps,' the pleasant Boulevards, the then so amiable People, all contributed to the effect this Song had upon me; anyhow, it has constantly revisited my memory for these forty-three years; and I was thinking, the other day, touched me more than any of Béranger's most beautiful Things. This, however, may be only one of 'Old Fitz's' Crotchets, as Tennyson and others would call them. [31]

I have been trying again at another Great *Artist's* work which I never could care for at all, Goethe's *Faust*, in Hayward's Prose Translation; Eighth Edition. Hayward quotes from Goethe himself, that, though of course much of a Poem must evaporate in a Prose Translation, yet the Essence must remain. Well; I distinguish as little of that Essential Poetry in the Faust now as when I first read it—longer ago than '*Le Bon Pasteur*,' and in other subsequent Attempts. I was tempted to think this was some Defect—great Defect—in myself: but a Note at the end of the Volume informs me that a much greater Wit than I was in the same plight—even Coleridge; who admires the perfect German Diction, the Songs, Choruses, etc. (which are such parts as cannot be translated into Prose); he also praises Margaret and Mephistopheles; but thinks Faust himself dull, and great part of the Drama flat and tiresome; and the whole Thing not a self-evolving Whole, but an unconnected Series of Scenes: all which are parts that can be judged of from Translation, by Goethe's own Authority. I find a great want of Invention and Imagination both in the Events and Characters.

Gervinus' Theory of Hamlet is very staking. Perhaps Shakespeare himself would have admitted, without ever having expressly designed, it. I always said with regard to the Explanation of Hamlet's Madness or Sanity, that Shakespeare himself might not have known the Truth any more than we understand the seeming Discords we see in People we know best. Shakespeare intuitively imagined, and portrayed, the Man without being able to give a reason—*perhaps*—I believe in Genius doing this: and remain your Inexhaustible Correspondent

E. F.G.

Excuse this very bad writing, which I have gone over 'with the pen of Correction,' and would have wholly re-written if my Eyes were not be-glared with the Sun on the River. You need only read the first part about Donne.

XIII.

[1873.]

DEAR MRS. KEMBLE,

Had you but written your Dublin Address in full, I should have caught you before you left. As you did not, I follow your Directions, and enclose to Coutts.

You see which of the three Photos I prefer—and very much prefer—by the two which I return: I am very much obliged to you indeed for taking all the

Trouble; and the Photo I have retained is very satisfactory to me in every respect: as I believe you will find it to be to such other Friends as you would give a Copy to. I can fancy that this Photo is a fair one; I mean, a fair Likeness: one of the full Faces was nearly as good to me, but for the darkness of the Lips—that common default in these things—but the other dark Fullface is very unfair indeed. You must give Copies to dear old Donne, and to one or two others, and I should like to hear from you [before you] leave England which they prefer.

It was indeed so unlike your obstinate habit of Reply—this last exception—that I thought you must be ill; and I was really thinking of writing to Mr. Leigh to ask about you—I have been ailing myself with some form of Rheumatism—whether Lumbago, Sciatica, or what not—which has made my rising up and sitting down especially uncomfortable; Country Doctor quite incompetent, etc. But the Heavenly Doctor, Phœbus, seems more efficient—especially now he has brought the Wind out of N.E.

I had meant to send you the Air of the Bon Pasteur when I sent the words: I never heard it but that once, but I find that the version you send me is almost identical with my Recollection of it. There is little merit in the Tune, except the pleasant resort to the Major at the two last Verses. I can now hear the Organist's *burr* at the closing 'Benira.'

I happened the other day on some poor little Verses [34a] which poor Haydon found of his poor Wife's writing in the midst of the Distress from which he extricated himself so suddenly. And I felt how these poor Verses touched me far more than any of Béranger's—though scarcely more than many of Burns'. I know that the Story which they involve appeals more to one's heart than the Frenchman does; but I am also sure that his perfect *Art* injures, and not assists, the utterance of Nature. I transcribe these poor Verses for you, as you may not have the Book at hand, and yet I think you will thank me for recalling them to you. I find them in a MS. Book I have which I call 'Half Hours with the Worst Authors,' [34b] and if People would believe that I know what is good for them in these matters, the Book would make a very good one for the Public. But if People don't see as I do by themselves, they wouldn't any the more for my telling them, not having any Name to bid their Attention. So my Bad Authors must be left to my Heirs and Assigns; as your Good Memoirs!

On second Thoughts, I shall (in spite of your Directions) keep two of the Photos: returning you only the hateful dark one. That is, I shall keep the twain, unless you desire me to return you one of them. Anyhow, do write to me before you go quite away, and believe me always yours

E. F.G.

XIV.

WOODBRIDGE: *Nov*. 18/73.

DEAR MRS. KEMBLE,

I should have written to you before, but that I was waiting for some account, for better or worse, of our friend Donne; who has been seriously ill this Fortnight and more. I don't know what his original Ailment was, unless a Cold; but the Effect has been to leave him so weak, that even now the Doctor fears for any Relapse which he might not be strong enough to bear. He had been for a Visit to friends in the West of England: and became ill directly he returned to London. You may think it odd I don't know what was his Illness; but Mowbray, who has told me all I know, did not tell me that: and so I did not ask, as I could do no good by knowing. Perhaps it is simply a Decay, or Collapse, of Body, or Nerves—or even Mind:—a Catastrophe which I never thought unlikely with Donne, who has toiled and suffered so much, for others rather than for himself; and keeping all his Suffering to himself. He wrote me a letter about himself a week ago; cheerful, and telling me of Books he read: so as no one would guess he was so ill; but a Letter from Mowbray by the same Post told me he was still in a precarious Condition. I had wished to tell you that he was better, if not well: but I may wait some time for that: and so I will write now:—with the Promise that I will write again directly there is anything else to tell.

Here my Reader comes to give me an Instalment of Tichborne: so I shall shut up, perhaps till To-morrow.

The Lord Chief Justice and Co. have just decided to adjourn the Trial for ten Days, till Witnesses arrive from your side of the Atlantic. My Reader has just adjourned to some Cake and Porter—I tell him not to hurry— while I go on with this Letter. To tell you that, I might almost have well adjourned writing 'sine die' (can you construe?), for I don't think I have more to tell you now. Only that I am reading—Crabbe! And I want you to tell me if he is read on that side of the Atlantic from which we are expecting Tichborne Witnesses.

(Reader finishes Cake and Porter: and we now adjourn to 'All the Year Round.')

10 p.m. 'All the Year Round' read—part of it—and Reader departed.

Pray do tell me if any one reads Crabbe in America; nobody does here, you know, but myself; who bore about it. Does Mrs. Wister, who reads many things? Does Mrs. Kemble, now she has the Atlantic between her and the old Country?

'Over the Forth I look to the North,
   But what is the North and its Hielands to me?
The North and the East gie small ease to my breast,
   The far foreign land and the wide rolling Sea.' [37]

I think that last line will bring the Tears into Mrs. Kemble's Eyes—which I can't find in the Photograph she sent me. Yet they are not extinguisht, surely?

I read in some Athenæum that A. Tennyson was changing his Publisher again: and some one told me that it was in consequence of the resigning Publisher having lost money by his contract with the Poet; which was, to pay him £1000 per Quarter for the exclusive sale of his Poems. It was a Woodbridge *Literati* who told me this, having read it in a Paper called 'The Publisher.' More I know not.

A little more such stuff I might write: but I think here is enough of it. For this Night, anyhow: so I shall lick the Ink from my Pen; and smoke one Pipe, not forgetting you while I do so; and if nothing turns up To-morrow, here is my Letter done, and I remaining yours always sincerely

E. F.G.

XV.

WOODBRIDGE: *Nov.* 24, [1873].

DEAR MRS. KEMBLE,

A note from Mowbray to-day says 'I think I can report the Father really on the road to recovery.'

So, as I think you will be as glad to know this as I am, I write again over the Atlantic. And, after all, you mayn't be over the Atlantic, but in London itself! Donne would have told me: but I don't like to trouble him with Questions, or writing of any sort. If you be in London, you will hear somehow of all this matter: if in America, my Letter won't go in vain.

Mowbray wrote me some while ago of the Death of your Sister's Son in the Hunting-field. [38] Mowbray said, aged thirty, I think: I had no idea, so old: born when I was with Thackeray in Coram Street—(*Jorum* Street, he called it) where I remember Mrs. Sartoris coming in her Brougham to bid him to Dinner, 1843.

I wrote to Annie Thackeray yesterday: politely telling her I couldn't relish her Old Kensington a quarter as much as her Village on the Cliff: which, however, I doat on. I still purpose to read Miss Evans: but my Instincts are against her—I mean, her Books.

What have you done with your Memoirs? Pollock is about to edit Macready's. And Chorley—have you read him? I shall devour him in time—that is, when Mudie will let me.

I wonder if there are Water-cresses in America, as there are on my tea-table while I write?

What do you think of these two lines which Crabbe didn't print?

> 'The shapeless purpose of a Soul that feels,
> And half suppresses Wrath, [39] and half reveals.'

My little bit of Good News about our Friend is the only reason and Apology for this Letter from

Yours ever and always
E. F.G.

XVI.

LOWESTOFT: *Febr.* 10/74.

DEAR MRS. KEMBLE,

A Letter to be written to you from the room I have written to you before in: but my Letter must wait till I return to Woodbridge, where your Address is on record. I have thought several times of writing to you since this Year began; but I have been in a muddle—leaving my old Markethill Lodgings, and vacillating between my own rather lonely Château, and this Place, where some Nieces are. I had wished to tell you what I know of our dear Donne: who Mowbray says gets on still. I suppose he will never be so strong again. Laurence wrote me that he had met him in the Streets, looking thinner (!) with (as it were) keener Eyes. That is a Portrait Painter's observation: probably a just one. Laurence has been painting for me a Copy of Pickersgill's Portrait of Crabbe—but I am afraid has made some muddle of it, according to his wont. I asked for a Sketch: he *will* elaborate—and spoil. Instead of copying the Colours he sees and could simply match on his Palette, he *will* puzzle himself as to whether the Eyebrows were once sandy, though now gray; and wants to compare Pickersgill's Portrait with Phillips'—which I particularly wished to be left out of account. Laurence is a dear little fellow—a Gentleman—Spedding said, 'made of Nature's very finest Clay.' [40] So he is: but the most obstinate little man—'incorrigible,' Richmond called him; and so he wearies out those who wish most to serve and employ him; and so has spoiled his own Fortune.

Do you read in America of Holman Hunt's famous new Picture of 'The Shadow of Death,' which he has been some seven Years painting—in Jerusalem, and now exhibits under theatrical Lights and accompaniments? This does not induce me to believe in H. Hunt more than heretofore: which is—not at all. Raffaelle, Mozart, Shakespeare, did not take all that time about a work, nor brought it forth to the world with so much Pomp and Circumstance.

Do you know Sainte Beuve's Causeries? I think one of the most delightful Books—a Volume of which I brought here, and makes me now write of it to you. It is a Book worth having—worth buying—for you can read it more than once, and twice. And I have taken up Don Quixote again: more Evergreen still; in Spanish, as it must be read, I doubt.

Here is a Sheet of Paper already filled, with matters very little worthy of sending over the Atlantic. But you will be glad of the Donne news, at any rate. Do tell me ever so little of yourself in return.

Now my Eyes have had enough of this vile steel pen; and so have yours, I should think: and I will mix a Glass of poor Sherry and Water, and fill a Pipe, and think of you while I smoke it. Think of me sometimes as

Yours always sincerely,
E. F.G.

P.S. I shall venture this Letter with no further Address than I remember now.

XVII.

LITTLE GRANGE: WOODBRIDGE, *May* 2/74.

DEAR MRS. KEMBLE,

My Castle Clock has gone 9 p.m., and I myself am but half an hour home from a Day to Lowestoft. Why I should begin a Letter to you under these circumstances I scarce know. However, I have long been intending to write: nay, actually did write half a Letter which I mislaid. What I wanted to tell you was—and is—that Donne is going on very well: Mowbray thinks he may be pronounced 'recovered.' You may have heard about him from some other hand before this: I know you will be glad to hear it at any time, from any quarter.

This my Castle had been named by me 'Grange Farm,' being formerly a dependency of a more considerable Château on the hill above. But a fine tall Woman, who has been staying two days, ordered me to call it 'Little Grange.' So it must be. She came to meet a little Niece of mine: both

Annies: one tall as the other is short: both capital in Head and Heart: I knew they would *fadge* well: so they did: so we all did, waiting on ourselves and on one another. Odd that I have another tip-top Annie on my small list of Acquaintances—Annie Thackeray.

I wonder what Spring is like in America. We have had an April of really 'magnifique' Weather: but here is that vixen May with its N.E. airs. A Nightingale however sings so close to my Bedroom that (the window being open) the Song is almost too loud.

I thought you would come back to Nightingale-land!

Donne is better: and Spedding has at last (I hear) got his load of Bacon off his Shoulders, after carrying it for near Forty years! Forty years long! A fortnight ago there was such a delicious bit of his in Notes and Queries, [42] a Comment on some American Comment on a passage in Antony and Cleopatra, that I recalled my old Sorrow that he had not edited Shakespeare long ago instead of wasting Life in washing his Blackamoor. Perhaps there is time for this yet: but is there the Will?

Pray, Madam, how do you emphasize the line—

'After Life's fitful Fever he sleeps well,'

which, by the by, one wonders never to have seen in some Churchyard? What do you think of this for an Epitaph—from Crabbe?—

'Friend of the Poor—the Wretched—the Betray'd,
They cannot pay thee—but thou shalt be paid.' [43]

This is a poor Letter indeed to make you answer—as answer you will—I really only intended to tell you of Donne; and remain ever yours

E. F.G.

Pollock is busy editing Macready's Papers.

XVIII.

LOWESTOFT: *June* 2/74.

DEAR MRS. KEMBLE,

Many a time have I written to you from this place: which may be the reason why I write again now—the very day your Letter reaches me—for I don't know that I have much to say, nor anything worth forcing from you the Answer that you will write. Let me look at your Letter again. Yes: so I thought of '*he* sleeps well,' and yet I do not remember to have heard it so read. (I never heard you read the Play) I don't think Macready read it so. I liked his Macbeth, I must say: only he would say 'Amen st-u-u-u-ck in his throat,' which was not only a blunder, but a vulgar blunder, I think.

Spedding—I should think indeed it was too late for him to edit Shakespeare, if he had not gone on doing so, as it were, all his Life. Perhaps it is too late for him to remember half, or a quarter, of his own Observations. Well then: I wish he would record what he does remember: if not an Edition of Shakespeare yet so many Notes toward an Edition. I am persuaded that no one is more competent. [45a]

You see your Americans will go too far. It was some American Professor's Note [45b] on 'the Autumn of his Bounty' which occasioned Spedding's delightful Comment some while ago, and made me remember my old wish that he should do the thing. But he will not: especially if one asks him.

Donne—Archdeacon Groome told me a Fortnight ago that he had been at Weymouth Street. Donne better, but still not his former Self.

By the by, I have got a Skeleton of my own at last: Bronchitis—which came on me a month ago—which I let go on for near three weeks—then was forced to call in a Doctor to subdue, who kept me a week indoors. And now I am told that, every Cold I catch, my Skeleton is to come out, etc. Every N.E. wind that blows, etc. I had not been shut up indoors for some fifty-five years—since Measles at school—but I had green before my Windows, and Don Quixote for Company within. *Que voulez-vous?*

Shakespeare again. A Doctor Whalley, who wrote a Tragedy for Mrs. Siddons (which she declined), proposed to her that she should read—'But screw your Courage to the *sticking place*,' with the appropriate action of using the Dagger. I think Mrs. Siddons good-naturedly admits there may be something in the suggestion. One reads this in the last memoir of Madame Piozzi, edited by Mr. Hayward.

Blackbird v. *Nightingale*. I have always loved the first best: as being so jolly, and the Note so proper from that golden Bill of his. But one does not like to go against received opinion. Your *Oriole* has been seen in these parts by old—very old—people: at least, a gay bird so named. But no one ever pretends to see him now.

Now have you perversely crossed the Address which you desire me to abide by: and I can't be sure of your 'Branchtown'? But I suppose that enough is clear to make my Letter reach you if it once gets across the Atlantic. And now this uncertainty about your writing recalls to me—very absurdly—an absurd Story told me by a pious, but humorous, man, which will please you if you don't know it already.

Scene.—Country Church on Winter's Evening. Congregation, with the Old Hundredth ready for the Parson to give out some Dismissal Words.

Good old Parson, not at all meaning rhyme, 'The Light has grown so very dim, I scarce can see to read the Hymn.'

Congregation, taking it up: to the first half of the Old Hundredth—

> 'The Light has grown so very dim,
> I scarce can see to read the Hymn.'

(Pause, as usual: *Parson*, mildly impatient) 'I did not mean to read a Hymn; I only meant my Eyes were dim.'

Congregation, to second part of Old Hundredth:—

> 'I did not mean to read a Hymn;
> I only meant my Eyes were dim.'

Parson, out of Patience, etc.:—

> 'I didn't mean a Hymn at all,—
> I think the Devil's in you all.'

I say, if you don't know this, it is worth your knowing, and making known over the whole Continent of America, North and South. And I am your trusty and affectionate old Beadsman (left rather deaf with that blessed Bronchitis)

E. F.G.

XIX.

LITTLE GRANGE: WOODBRIDGE, *July* 21, [1874.]

DEAR MRS. KEMBLE,

I must write to you—for I have seen Donne, and can tell you that he looks and seems much better than I had expected, though I had been told to expect well: he was upright, well coloured, animated; I should say (*sotto voce*) better than he seemed to me two years ago. And this in spite of the new Lord Chamberlain [48a] having ousted him from his Theatrical post, wanting a younger and more active man to go and see the Plays, as well as read them. I do not think this unjust; I was told by Pollock that the dismissal was rather abrupt: but Donne did not complain of it. When does he complain? He will now, however, leave Weymouth Street, and inhabit some less costly house—not wanting indeed so large [a] one for his present household. He is shortly going with his Daughters to join the Blakesleys at Whitby. Mowbray was going off for his Holiday to Cornwall: I just heard him speaking of Freddy's present Address to his father: Blanche was much stronger, from the treatment of a Dr. Beard [48b] (I think). I was quite moved by her warm salutation when I met her, after some fifteen years' absence. All this I report from a Visit I made to Donne's own house in London. A thing I scarce ever thought to do again, you may know: but I could not bear to be close to him in London for two days without assuring myself with my own Eyes how he looked. I think I observed a slight hesitation of memory: but certainly not so much as I find in myself, nor, I suppose, unusual in one's Contemporaries. My visit to London followed a visit to Edinburgh: which I have intended these thirty years, only for the purpose of seeing my dear Sir Walter's House and Home: and which I am glad to have seen, as that of Shakespeare. I had expected to find a rather Cockney Castle: but no such thing: all substantially and proportionably built, according to the Style of the Country: the Grounds well and simply laid out: the woods he planted well-grown, and that dear Tweed running and murmuring still—as on the day of his Death. [49a] I did not so much care for Melrose, and Jedburgh, [49b] though his Tomb is there—in one of the half-ruined corners. Another day I went to Trossachs, Katrine, Lomond, etc., which (as I expected) seemed much better to me in Pictures and Drop-scenes. I was but three days in Scotland, and was glad to get back to my own dull flat country, though I did worship the Pentland, Cheviot, and Eildon, Hills, more for their Associations than themselves. They are not big enough for that.

I saw little in London: the Academy Pictures even below the average, I thought: only a Picture by Millais of an old Sea Captain [49c] being read to by his Daughter which moistened my Eyes. I thought she was reading him the Bible, which he seemed half listening to, half rambling over his past Life: but I am told (I had no Catalogue) that she was reading about the North West Passage. There were three deep of Bonnets before Miss Thompson's famous Roll Call of the Guards in the Crimea; so I did not wait till they fell away. [50a]

Yours always

E. F.G.

XX.

LOWESTOFT: *Aug.* 24, [1874.]

DEAR MRS. KEMBLE,

Your letter reached me this morning: and you see I lose no time in telling you that, as I hear from Pollock, Donne is allowed £350 a year retiring Pension. So I think neither he nor his friends have any reason to complain. His successor in the office is named (I think) 'Piggott' [50b]—Pollock thinks a good choice. Lord Hertford brought the old and the new Examiners together to Dinner: and all went off well. Perhaps Donne himself may have told you all this before now. He was to be, about this time, with the Blakesleys at Whitby or Filey. I have not heard any of these particulars from himself: nothing indeed since I saw him in London.

Pollock was puzzled by an entry in Macready's Journal—1831 or 1832—'Received Thackeray's Tragedy' with some such name as 'Retribution.' I told Pollock I was sure it was not W. M. T., who (especially at that time) had more turn to burlesque than real Tragedy: and sure that he would have told me of it then, whether accepted or rejected—as rejected it was. Pollock thought for some while that, in spite of the comic Appearance we keep up, we should each of us rise up from the Grave with a MS. Tragedy in our hands, etc. However, he has become assured it was some other Thackeray: I suppose one mentioned by Planché as a Dramatic *Dilettante*—of the same Family, I think, as W. M. T.

Spedding has sent me the concluding Volume of his Bacon: the final summing up simple, noble, deeply pathetic—rather on Spedding's own Account than his Hero's, for whose Vindication so little has been done by the sacrifice of forty years of such a Life as Spedding's. Positively, nearly all the new matter which S. has produced makes against, rather than for, Bacon: and I do think the case would have stood better if Spedding had only argued from the old materials, and summed up his Vindication in one small Volume some thirty-five years ago.

I have been sunning myself in Dickens—even in his later and very inferior 'Mutual Friend,' and 'Great Expectations'—Very inferior to his best: but with things better than any one else's best, caricature as they may be. I really must go and worship at Gadshill, as I have worshipped at Abbotsford, though with less Reverence, to be sure. But I must look on Dickens as a mighty Benefactor to Mankind. [52]

This is shamefully bad writing of mine—very bad manners, to put any one—especially a Lady—to the trouble and pain of deciphering. I hope all about Donne is legible, for you will be glad of it. It is Lodging-house Pens and Ink that is partly to blame for this scrawl. Now, don't answer till I write you something better: but believe me ever and always yours

E. F.G.

XXI.

DEAR MRS. KEMBLE,

Do, pray, write your Macready (Thackeray used to say 'Megreedy') Story to Pollock: Sir F. 59 Montagu Square. I rather think he was to be going to Press with his Megreedy about this time: but you may be sure he will deal with whatever you may confide to him discreetly and reverently. It is 'Miladi' P. who worshipped Macready: and I think I never recovered what Esteem I had with her when I told her I could not look on him as a 'Great' Actor at all. I see in Planché's Memoirs that when your Father prophesied great things of him to your Uncle J. P. K., the latter said, '*Con quello viso?*' which '*viso*' did very well however in parts not positively heroic. But one can't think of him along with Kean, who was heroic in spite of undersize. How he swelled up in Othello! I remember thinking he looked almost as tall as your Father when he came to Silence that dreadful Bell.

I think you agree with me about Kean: remembering your really capital Paper—in *Macmillan* [53a]—about Dramatic and Theatric. I often look to that Paper, which is bound up with some Essays by other Friends— Spedding among them—no bad Company. I was thinking of your Pasta story of 'feeling' the Antique, etc., [53b] when reading in my dear Ste. Beuve [53c] of my dear Madame du Deffand asking Madame de Choiseul: 'You *know* you love me, but do you *feel* you love me?' '*Quoi? vous m'aimez donc?*' she said to her secretary Wiart, when she heard him sobbing as she dictated her last letter to Walpole. [53d]

All which reminds me of one of your friends departed—Chorley—whose Memoirs one now buys from Mudie for 2*s.* 6*d.* or so. And well—*well*— worth to those who recollect him. I only knew him by Face—and Voice— at your Father's, and your Sister's: and used to think what a little waspish *Dilettante* it was: and now I see he was something very much better indeed: and I only hope I may have Courage to face my Death as he had. Dickens loved him, who did not love Humbugs: and Chorley would have two strips of Gadshill Yew [54] put with him in his Coffin. Which again reminds me that—*à propos* of your comments on Dickens' crimson waistcoat, etc., Thackeray told me thirty years ago, that Dickens did it, not from any idea of Cockney fashion: but from a veritable passion for Colours—which I can well sympathize with, though I should not exhibit them on my own Person—for very good reasons. Which again reminds me of what you write about my abiding the sight of you in case you return to England next year. Oh, my dear Mrs. Kemble, you must know how wrong all that is— *tout au contraire*, in fact. Tell me a word about Chorley when next you write:

you said once that Mendelssohn laughed at him: then, he ought not. How well I remember his strumming away at some Waltz in Harley or Wimpole's endless Street, while your Sister and a few other Guests went round. I thought then he looked at one as if thinking 'Do you think me then—a poor, red-headed Amateur, as Rogers does?' That old Beast! I don't scruple to say so.

I am positively looking over my everlasting Crabbe again: he naturally comes in about the Fall of the Year. Do you remember his wonderful 'October Day'? [55]

> 'Before the Autumn closed,
> When Nature, ere her Winter Wars, reposed
> When from our Garden, as we looked above,
> No Cloud was seen; and nothing seem'd to move;
> When the wide River was a Silver Sheet,
> And upon Ocean slept the unanchor'd fleet:
> When the wing'd Insect settled in our Sight,
> And waited Wind to recommence her flight.'

And then, the Lady who believes her young Lover dead, and has vowed eternal Celibacy, sees him advancing, a portly, well to do, middle aged man: and swears she won't have him: and does have him, etc.

Which reminds me that I want you to tell me if people in America read Crabbe.

Farewell, dear Mrs. Kemble, for the present: always yours

E. F.G.

Have you the Robin in America? One is singing in the little bit Garden before me now.

XXII.

59 MONTAGU SQUARE, LONDON, W.
5 *Oct.*/74.

MY DEAR FITZ,

It is very good of Mrs. Kemble to wish to tell me a story about Macready, and I shall be glad to know it.

Only—she should know that I am not writing his life—but editing his autobiographical reminiscences and diaries—and unless the anecdote could be introduced to explain or illustrate these, it would not be serviceable for my present purpose.

But for its own sake and for Macready's I should like to be made acquainted with it.

I am making rapid way with the printing—in fact have got to the end of what will be Vol. I. in slip—so that I hope the work may be out by or soon after Christmas, if the engravings are also ready by that time.

It will be, I am sure, most interesting—and will surprise a great many people who did not at all know what Macready really was.

You last heard of me at Clovelly—where we spent a delightful month— more rain than was pleasant—but on the whole charming. I think I told you that Annie Thackeray was there for a night—and that we bound her over not to make the reading public too well acquainted with the place, which would not be good for it.

Since then—a fortnight at St. Julians—and the same time at Tunbridge Wells—I coming up to town three times a week—

> Noctes atque dies patet atri janua Ditis, [56]

and as there are other points of resemblance—so it is natural that the Gates of Justice should be open even during the Vacation—just a little ajar—with somebody to look after it, which somebody it has been my lot to be this year.

T. Wells was very pleasant—I like the old-fashioned place—and can always people the Pantiles (they call it the Parade now) with Dr. Johnson and the Duchess of Kingston, and the Bishop of Salisbury and the foreign baron, and the rest. [57a]

Miladi and Walter are at Paris for a few days. I am keeping house with Maurice—Yours, W. F. P^k.

We have J. S.'s [57b] seventh volume—and I am going to read it—but do not know where he is himself. I have not seen the 'white, round object—which is the head of him' for some time past—not since—July.—

XXIII.

WOODBRIDGE: *Nov*. 17/74.

DEAR MRS. KEMBLE,

Your Letter about Megreedy, as Thackeray used to call him, is very interesting: I mean as connected with your Father also. Megreedy, with all his flat face, managed to look well as Virginius, didn't he? And, as I thought, well enough in Macbeth, except where he *would* stand with his mouth open (after the Witches had hailed him), till I longed to pitch something into it out of the Pit, the dear old Pit. How came *he* to play Henry IV. instead of your Father, in some Play I remember at C. G., though I did not see it? How well I remember your Father in Falconbridge (Young, K. John) as he looked sideway and upward before the Curtain fell on his Speech.

Then his Petruchio: I remember his looking up, as the curtain fell at the end, to where he knew that Henry had taken me—some very upper Box. And I remember too his standing with his Hunting spear, looking with pleasure at pretty Miss Foote as Rosalind. He played well what was natural to him: the gallant easy Gentleman—I thought his Charles Surface rather cumbrous: but he was no longer young.

Mrs. Wister quite mistook the aim of my Query about Crabbe: I asked if he were read in America for the very reason that he is not read in England. And in the October *Cornhill* is an Article upon him (I hope not by Leslie Stephen), so ignorant and self-sufficient that I am more wroth than ever. The old Story of 'Pope in worsted stockings'—why I could cite whole Paragraphs of as fine texture as Molière—incapable of Epigram, the Jackanapes says of 'our excellent Crabbe'—why I could find fifty of the very best Epigrams in five minutes. But now do you care for him? 'Honour bright?' as Sheridan used to say. I don't think I ever knew a Woman who did like C., except my Mother. What makes People (this stupid Reviewer among them) talk of worsted Stockings is because of having read only his earlier works: when he himself talked of his Muse as

'Muse of the Mad, the Foolish, and the Poor,' [59a]

the Borough: Parish Register, etc. But it is his Tales of the Hall which discover him in silk Stockings; the subjects, the Scenery, the Actors, of a more Comedy kind: with, I say, Paragraphs, and Pages, of fine Molière style—only too often defaced by carelessness, disproportion, and 'longueurs' intolerable. I shall leave my Edition of Tales of the Hall, made legible by the help of Scissors and Gum, with a word or two of Prose to bridge over pages of stupid Verse. I don't wish to try and supersede the Original, but, by the Abstract, to get People to read the whole, and so learn (as in Clarissa) how to get it all under command. I even wish that some one in America would undertake to publish—in whole, or part by part— my 'Readings in Crabbe,' viz., Tales of the Hall: but no one would let me do the one thing I can do.

I think you must repent having encouraged such a terrible Correspondent as myself: you have the remedy in your own hands, you know. I find that the Bronchitis I had in Spring returns upon me now: so I have to give up my Night walks, and stalk up and down my own half-lighted Hall (like Chateaubriand's Father) [59b] till my Reader comes. Ever yours truly

E. F.G.

Nov. 21.

I detained this letter till I heard from Donne, who has been at Worthing, and writes cheerfully.

XXIV.

LOWESTOFT, *Febr.* 11/75.

DEAR MRS. KEMBLE,

Will you please to thank Mr. Furness for the trouble he has taken about Crabbe. The American Publisher is like the English, it appears, and both may be quite right. They certainly are right in not accepting anything except on very good recommendation; and a Man's Fame is the best they can have for that purpose. I should not in the least be vext or even disappointed at any rejection of my Crabbe, but it is not worth further trouble to any party to send across the Atlantic what may, most probably, be returned with thanks and Compliments. And then Mr. Furness would feel bound to ask some other Publisher, and you to write to me about it. No, no! Thank him, if you please: you know I thank you: and then I will let the matter drop.

The Athenæum told me there was a Paper by Carlyle in the January Fraser—on the old Norway Kings. Then People said it was not his: but his it is, surely enough (though I have no Authority but my own Judgment for saying so), and quite delightful. If missing something of his Prime, missing also all his former 'Sound and Fury,' etc., and as alive as ever. I had thoughts of writing to him on the subject, but have not yet done so. But pray do you read the Papers: there is a continuation in the February Fraser: and 'to be continued' till ended, I suppose.

Your Photograph—Yes—I saw your Mother in it, as I saw her in you when you came to us in Woodbridge in 1852. That is, I saw her such as I had seen her in a little sixpenny Engraving in a 'Cottage Bonnet,' something such as you wore when you stept out of your Chaise at the Crown Inn.

My Mother always said that your Mother was by far the most witty, sensible, and agreeable Woman she knew. I remember one of the very few delightful Dinner parties I ever was at—in St. James' Place—(was it?) a Party of seven or eight, at a round Table, your Mother at the head of the Table, and Mrs. F. Kemble my next Neighbour. And really the (almost) only other pleasant Dinner was one you gave me and the Donnes in Savile Row, before going to see Wigan in 'Still Waters,' which you said was *your* Play, in so far as you had suggested the Story from some French Novel.

I used to think what a deep current of melancholy was under your Mother's Humour. Not 'under,' neither: for it came up as naturally to the surface as her Humour. My mother always said that one great charm in her was, her Naturalness.

If you read to your Company, pray do you ever read *the* Scene in the 'Spanish Tragedy' quoted in C. Lamb's Specimens—such a Scene as (not being in Verse, and quite familiar talk) I cannot help reading to my Guests—very few and far between—I mean by 'I,' one who has no gift at all for reading except the feeling of a few things: and I can't help stumbling upon Tears in this. Nobody knows who wrote this one scene: it was thought Ben Jonson, who could no more have written it than I who read it: for what else of his is it like? Whereas, Webster one fancies might have done it. It is not likely that you do not know this wonderful bit: but, if you have it not by heart almost, look for it again at once, and make others do so by reading to them.

The enclosed Note from Mowbray D[onne] was the occasion of my writing thus directly to you. And yet I have spoken 'de omnibus other rebus' first. But I venture to think that your feeling on the subject will be pretty much like my own, and so, no use in talking.

Now, if I could send you part of what I am now packing up for some Woodbridge People—some—some—Saffron Buns!—for which this Place is notable from the first day of Lent till Easter—A little Hamper of these!

Now, my dear Mrs. Kemble, do consider this letter of mine as an Answer to yours—your two—else I shall be really frightened at making you write so often to yours always and sincerely

E. F.G.

XXV.

LOWESTOFT, *March* 11/75.

DEAR MRS. KEMBLE,

I am really ashamed that you should apologize for asking me a Copy of Calderon, etc. [64a] I had about a hundred Copies of all those things printed *when* printed: and have not had a hundred friends to give them to—poor Souls!—and am very well pleased to give to any one who likes—especially any Friend of yours. I think however that your reading of them has gone most way to make your Lady ask. But, be that as it may, I will send you a Copy directly I return to my own Château, which I mean to do when the Daffodils have taken the winds of March. [64b]

We have had severe weather here: it has killed my Brother Peter (not John, my eldest) who tried to winter at Bournemouth, after having wintered for the last ten years at Cannes. Bronchitis:—which (*sotto voce*) I have as yet kept Cold from coming to. But one knows one is not 'out of the Wood' yet; May, if not March, being, you know, one of our worst Seasons.

I heard from our dear Donne a week ago; speaking with all his own blind and beautiful Love for his lately lost son; and telling me that he himself keeps his heart going by Brandy. But he speaks of this with no Fear at all. He is going to leave Weymouth Street, but when, or for where, he does not say. He spoke of a Letter he had received from you some while ago.

Now about Crabbe, which also I am vext you should have trouble about. I wrote to you the day after I had your two Letters, with Mr. Furness' enclosed, and said that, seeing the uncertainty of any success in the matter, I really would not bother you or him any more. You know it is but a little thing; which, even if a Publisher tried piece-meal, would very likely be scouted: I only meant 'piece-meal,' by instalments: so as they could be discontinued if not liked. But I suppose I must keep my Work—of paste, and scissors—for the benefit of the poor Friends who have had the benefit of my other Works.

Well: as I say, I wrote and posted my Letter at once, asking you to thank Mr. Furness for me. I think this must be a month ago—perhaps you had my Letter the day after you posted this last of yours, dated February 21. Do not trouble any more about it, pray: read Carlyle's 'Kings of Norway' in Fraser and believe me ever yours

E. F.G.

I will send a little bound Copy of the Plays for yourself, dear Mrs. Kemble, if you will take them; so you can give the Lady those you have:—but, whichever way you like.

XXVI.

LOWESTOFT, *March* 17/75.

DEAR MRS. KEMBLE,

This bit of Letter is written to apprise you that, having to go to Woodbridge three days ago, I sent you by Post a little Volume of the Plays, and (what I had forgotten) a certain little Prose Dialogue [65] done up with them. This is more than you wanted, but so it is. The Dialogue is a pretty thing in some respects: but disfigured by some confounded *smart* writing in parts: And this is all that needs saying about the whole concern. You must not think necessary to say anything more about it yourself, only that you receive the Book. If you do not, in a month's time, I shall suppose it has somehow lost its way over the Atlantic: and then I will send you the Plays you asked for, stitched together—and those only.

I hope you got my Letter (which you had not got when your last was written) about Crabbe: for I explained in it why I did not wish to trouble you or Mr. Furness any more with such an uncertain business. Anyhow, I must ask you to thank him for the trouble he had already taken, as I hope you know that I thank you also for your share in it.

I scarce found a Crocus out in my Garden at home, and so have come back here till some green leaf shows itself. We are still under the dominion of North East winds, which keep people coughing as well as the Crocus under ground. Well, we hope to earn all the better Spring by all this Cold at its outset.

I have so often spoken of my fear of troubling you by all my Letters, that I won't say more on that score. I have heard no news of Donne since I wrote. I have been trying to read Gil Blas and La Fontaine again; but, as before, do not relish either. [67] I must get back to my Don Quixote by and by.

Yours as ever

E. F.G.

I wonder if this letter will smell of Tobacco: for it is written just after a Pipe, and just before going to bed.

XXVII.

LOWESTOFT: *April* 9 / 75.

DEAR MRS. KEMBLE,

I wrote you a letter more than a fortnight ago—mislaid it—and now am rather ashamed to receive one from you thanking me beforehand for the mighty Book which I posted you a month ago. I only hope you will not feel bound to acknowledge [it] when it does reach you, I think I said so in the Letter I wrote to go along with it. And I must say no more in the way of deprecating your Letters, after what you write me. Be assured that all my deprecations were for your sake, not mine; but there's an end of them now.

I had a longish letter from Donne himself some while ago; indicating, I thought, *some* debility of Mind and Body. He said, however, he was going on very well. And a Letter from Mowbray (three or four days old) speaks of his Father as 'remarkably well.' But these Donnes won't acknowledge

Bodily any more than Mental fault in those they love. Blanche had been ill, of neuralgic Cold: Valentia not well: but both on the mending hand now.

It has been indeed the Devil of a Winter: and even now—To-day as I write—no better than it was three months ago. The Daffodils scarce dare take April, let alone March; and I wait here till a Green Leaf shows itself about Woodbridge.

I have been looking over four of Shakespeare's Plays, edited by Clark and Wright: editors of the 'Cambridge Shakespeare.' These 'Select Plays' are very well done, I think: Text, and Notes; although with somewhat too much of the latter. Hamlet, Macbeth, Tempest, and Shylock—I heard them talking in my room—all alive about me.

By the by—How did *you* read 'To-morrow and To-morrow, etc.' All the Macbeths I have heard took the opportunity to become melancholy when they came to this: and, no doubt, some such change from Fury and Desperation was a relief to the Actor, and perhaps to the Spectator. But I think it *should* all go in the same Whirlwind of Passion as the rest: Folly!—Stage Play!—Farthing Candle; Idiot, etc. Macready used to drop his Truncheon when he heard of the Queen's Death, and stand with his Mouth open for some while—which didn't become him.

I have not seen his Memoir: only an extract or two in the Papers. He always seemed to me an Actor by Art and Study, with some native Passion to inspire him. But as to Genius—we who have seen Kean!

I don't know if you were acquainted with Sir A. Helps, [68] whose Death (one of this Year's Doing) is much regretted by many. I scarcely knew him except at Cambridge forty years ago: and could never relish his Writings, amiable and sensible as they are. I suppose they will help to swell that substratum of Intellectual *Peat* (Carlyle somewhere calls it) [69] from [which] one or two living Trees stand out in a Century. So Shakespeare above all that Old Drama which he grew amidst, and which (all represented by him alone) might henceforth be left unexplored, with the exception of a few twigs of Leaves gathered here and there—as in Lamb's Specimens. Is Carlyle himself—with all his Genius—to subside into the Level? Dickens, with all his Genius, but whose Men and Women act and talk already after a more obsolete fashion than Shakespeare's? I think some of Tennyson will survive, and drag the deader part along with it, I suppose. And (I doubt) Thackeray's terrible Humanity.

And I remain yours ever sincerely,
A very small Peat-contributor,
E. F.G.

I am glad to say that Clark and Wright Bowdlerize Shakespeare, though much less extensively than Bowdler. But in one case, I think, they have gone further—altering, instead of omitting: which is quite wrong!

XXVIII.

LOWESTOFT: *April* 19/75.

DEAR MRS. KEMBLE,

Yesterday I wrote you a letter: enveloped it: then thought there was something in it you might misunderstand—Yes!—the written word across the Atlantic looking perhaps so different from what intended; so kept my Letter in my pocket, and went my ways. This morning your Letter of April 3 is forwarded to me; and I shall re-write the one thing that I yesterday wrote about—as I had intended to do before your Letter came. Only, let me say that I am really ashamed that you should have taken the trouble to write again about my little, little, Book.

Well—what I wrote about yesterday, and am to-day about to re-write, is— Macready's Memoirs. You asked me in your previous Letter whether I had read them. No—I had not: and had meant to wait till they came down to Half-price on the Railway Stall before I bought them. But I wanted to order something of my civil Woodbridge Bookseller: so took the course of ordering this Book, which I am now reading at Leisure: for it does not interest me enough to devour at once. It is however a very unaffected record of a very conscientious Man, and Artist; conscious (I think) that he was not a great Genius in his Profession, and conscious of his defect of Self-control in his Morals. The Book is almost entirely about *himself*, *his* Studies, *his* Troubles, *his* Consolations, etc.; not from Egotism, I do think, but as the one thing he had to consider in writing a Memoir and Diary. Of course one expects, and wishes, that the Man's self should be the main subject; but one also wants something of the remarkable people he lived with, and of whom one finds little here but that 'So-and-so came and went'—scarce anything of what they said or did, except on mere business; Macready seeming to have no Humour; no intuition into Character, no Observation of those about him (how could he be a great Actor then?)— Almost the only exception I have yet reached is his Account of Mrs. Siddons, whom he worshipped: whom he acted with in her later years at Country Theatres: and who was as kind to him as she was even then heart-rending on the Stage. He was her Mr. Beverley: [71] 'a very young husband,' she told him: but 'in the right way if he would study, study, study—and not marry till thirty.' At another time, when he was on the stage, she stood at the side scene, called out 'Bravo, Sir, Bravo!' and clapped her hands—all in sight of the Audience, who joined in her Applause. Macready also tells of her falling into such a Convulsion, as it were, in Aspasia [72a] (what a subject for such a sacrifice!) that the Curtain had to be dropped, and Macready's Father, and Holman, who were among the Audience, looked at each other to see which was whitest! This was the Woman whom people somehow came to look on as only majestic and terrible—I suppose, after Miss O'Neill rose upon her Setting.

Well, but what I wrote about yesterday—a passage about you yourself. I fancy that he and you were very unsympathetic: nay, you have told me of some of his Egotisms toward you, 'who had scarce learned the rudiments of your Profession' (as also he admits that he scarce had). But, however that may have been, his Diary records, 'Decr. 20 (1838) Went to Covent Garden Theatre: on my way continued the perusal of Mrs. Butler's Play, which is a work of uncommon power. Finished the reading of Mrs. Butler's Play, which is one of the most powerful of the modern Plays I have seen—most painful—almost shocking—but full of Power, Poetry and Pathos. She is one of the most remarkable women of the present Day.'

So you see that if he thought you deficient in the Art which you (like himself) had unwillingly to resort to, you were efficient in the far greater Art of supplying that material on which the Histrionic must depend. (N.B.—Which play of yours? Not surely the 'English Tragedy' unless shown to him in MS.? [72b] Come: I have sent you my Translations: you should give me your Original Plays. When I get home, I will send you an old Scratch by Thackeray of yourself in Louisa of Savoy—shall I?)

On the whole, I find Macready (so far as I have gone) a just, generous, religious, and affectionate Man; on the whole, humble too! One is well content to assure oneself of this; but it is not worth spending 28*s.* upon.

Macready would have made a better Scholar—or Divine—than Actor, I think: a Gentleman he would have been in any calling, I believe, in spite of his Temper—which he acknowledges, laments, and apologizes for, on reflection.

Now, here is enough of my small writing for your reading. I have been able to read, and admire, some Corneille lately: as to Racine—'*Ce n'est pas mon homme*,' as Catharine of Russia said of him. Now I am at Madame de Sévigné's delightful Letters; I should like to send you a Bouquet of Extracts: but must have done now, being always yours

E. F.G.

XXIX.

DEAR MRS. KEMBLE,

I have been wishing to send you Carlyle's Norway Kings, and oh! such a delightful Paper of Spedding's on the Text of Richard III. [74] But I have waited till I should hear from you, knowing that you *will* reply! And not feeling sure, till I hear, whether you are not on your way to England Eastward ho!—even as I am now writing!—Or, I fancy—should you not be well? Anyhow, I shall wait till some authentic news of yourself comes to me. I should not mind sending you Carlyle—why, yes! I *will* send him! But old Spedding—which is only a Proof—I won't send till I know that you are still where you were to receive it—Oh! such a piece of musical criticism! without the least pretence to being Musick: as dry as he can make it, in fact. But he does, with utmost politeness, smash the Cambridge Editors' Theory about the Quarto and Folio Text of R. III.—in a way that perhaps Mr. Furness might like to see.

Spedding says that Irving's Hamlet is simply—*hideous*—a strong expression for Spedding to use. But—(lest I should think his condemnation was only the Old Man's fault of depreciating all that is new), he extols Miss Ellen Terry's Portia as simply *a perfect Performance*: remembering (he says) all the while how fine was Fanny Kemble's. Now, all this you shall read for yourself, when I have token of your Whereabout, and Howabout: for I will send you Spedding's Letter, as well as his Paper.

Spedding won't go and see Salvini's Othello, because he does not know Italian, and also because he hears that Salvini's is a different Conception of Othello from Shakespeare's. I can't understand either reason; but Spedding is (as Carlyle [75a] wrote me of his Bacon) the 'invincible, and victorious.' At any rate, I can't beat him. Irving I never could believe in as Hamlet, after seeing part of his famous Performance of a Melodrama called 'The Bells' three or four years ago. But the Pollocks, and a large World beside, think him a Prodigy—whom Spedding thinks—a Monster! To this Complexion is the English Drama come.

I wonder if your American Winter has transformed itself to such a sudden Summer as here in Old England. I returned to my Woodbridge three weeks ago: not a leaf on the Trees: in ten days they were all green, and people—perspiring, I suppose one must say. Now again, while the Sun is quite as Hot, the Wind has swerved round to the East—so as one broils on one side and freezes on t'other—and I—the Great Twalmley [75b]—am keeping indoors from an Intimation of Bronchitis. I think it is time for one to leave the Stage oneself.

I heard from Mowbray Donne some little while ago; as he said nothing (I think) of his Father, I conclude that there is nothing worse of him to be said. He (the Father) has a Review of Macready—laudatory, I suppose—in the Edinburgh, and *Mr.* Helen Faucit (Martin) as injurious a one in the Quarterly: the reason of the latter being (it is supposed) because *Mrs.* H. F. is not noticed except just by name. To this Complexion also!

Ever   yours,
E. F.G.

Since writing as above, your Letter comes; as you do not speak of moving, I shall send Spedding and Carlyle by Post to you, in spite of the Loss of Income you tell me of which would (I doubt) close up *my* thoughts some while from such speculations. I do not think *you* will take trouble so to heart. Keep Spedding for me: Carlyle I don't want again. Tired as you— and I—are of Shakespeare Commentaries, you will like this.

XXX.

LOWESTOFT: *July* 22/75.

DEAR MRS. KEMBLE,

I have abstained from writing since you wrote me how busily your Pen was employed for the Press: I wished more than ever to spare you the trouble of answering me—which I knew you would not forgo. And now you will feel called upon, I suppose, though I would fain spare you.

Though I date from this place still, I have been away from it at my own Woodbridge house for two months and more; only returning here indeed to help make a better Holiday for a poor Lad who is shut up in a London Office while his Heart is all for Out-of-Door, Country, Sea, etc. We have been having wretched Holyday weather, to be sure: rain, mist, and wind; St. Swithin at his worst: but all better than the hateful London Office—to which he must return the day after To-morrow, poor Fellow!

I suppose you will see—if you have not yet seen—Tennyson's Q. Mary. I don't know what to say about it; but the Times says it is the finest Play since Shakespeare; and the Spectator that it is superior to Henry VIII. Pray do you say something of it, when you write:—for I think you must have read it before that time comes.

Then Spedding has written a delicious Paper in Fraser about the late Representation of The Merchant of Venice, and his E. Terry's perfect personation of his perfect Portia. I cannot agree with him in all he says— for one thing, I must think that Portia made 'a hole in her manners' when she left Antonio trembling for his Life while she all the while [knew] how to defeat the Jew by that knowledge of the Venetian Law which (oddly enough) the Doge knew nothing about. Then Spedding thinks that Shylock has been so pushed forward ever since Macklin's time as to preponderate over all the rest in a way that Shakespeare never intended. [77] But, if Shakespeare did not intend this, he certainly erred in devoting so much of his most careful and most powerful writing to a Character which he meant to be subsidiary, and not principal. But Spedding is more likely to be right than I: right or wrong he pleads his cause as no one else can. His Paper is in this July number of Fraser: I would send it you if you had more time for reading than your last Letter speaks of; I *will* send if you wish.

I have not heard of Donne lately: he had been staying at Lincoln with Blakesley, the Dean: and is now, I suppose, at Chislehurst, where he took a house for a month.

And I am yours ever and sincerely
E. F.G.

XXXI.

WOODBRIDGE, *Aug.* 24, [1875.]

Now, my dear Mrs. Kemble, you will have to call me 'a Good Creature,' as I have found out a Copy of your capital Paper, [78] and herewith post it to you. Had I not found this Copy (which Smith & Elder politely found for me) I should have sent you one of my own, cut out from a Volume of Essays by other friends, Spedding, etc., on condition that you should send me a Copy of such Reprint as you may make of it in America. It is extremely interesting; and I always think that your Theory of the Intuitive *versus* the Analytical and Philosophical applies to the other Arts as well as that of the Drama. Mozart couldn't tell how he made a Tune; even a whole Symphony, he said, unrolled itself out of a leading idea by no logical process. Keats said that no Poetry was worth [anything] unless it came spontaneously as Leaves to a Tree, etc. [79] I have no faith in your Works of Art done on Theory and Principle, like Wordsworth, Wagner, Holman Hunt, etc.

But, one thing you can do on Theory, and carry it well into Practice: which is—to write your Letter on Paper which does not let the Ink through, so that (according to your mode of paging) your last Letter was crossed: I really thought it so at first, and really had very hard work to make it out— some parts indeed still defying my Eyes. What I read of your remarks on Portia, etc., is so good that I wish to keep it: but still I think I shall enclose you a scrap to justify my complaint. It was almost by Intuition, not on Theory, that I deciphered what I did. Pray you amend this. My MS. is bad enough, and on that very account I would avoid diaphanous Paper. Are you not ashamed?

I shall send you Spedding's beautiful Paper on the Merchant of Venice [80] if I can lay hands on it: but at present my own room is given up to a fourth Niece (Angel that I am!) You would see that S[pedding] agrees with you about Portia, and in a way that I am sure must please you. But (so far as I can decipher that fatal Letter) you say nothing at all to me of the other Spedding Paper I sent to you (about the Cambridge Editors, etc.), which I must have back again indeed, unless you wish to keep it, and leave me to beg another Copy. Which to be sure I can do, and will, if your heart is set upon it—which I suppose it is not at all.

I have not heard of Donne for so long a time, that I am uneasy, and have written to Mowbray to hear. M[owbray] perhaps is out on his Holyday, else I think he would have replied at once. And 'no news may be the Good News.'

I have no news to tell of myself; I am much as I have been for the last four months: which is, a little ricketty. But I get out in my Boat on the River three or four hours a Day when possible, and am now as ever yours sincerely

E. F.G.

XXXII.

[*Oct.* 4, 1875]

DEAR MRS. KEMBLE,

I duly received your last legible Letter, and Spedding's Paper: for both of which all Thanks. But you must do something more for me. I see by Notes and Queries that you are contributing Recollections to some American Magazine; I want you to tell me where I can get this, with all the back Numbers in which you have written.

I return the expected favour (Hibernicé) with the enclosed Prints, one of which is rather a Curiosity: that of Mrs. Siddons by Lawrence when he was *ætat.* 13. The other, done from a Cast of herself by herself, is only remarkable as being almost a Copy of this early Lawrence—at least, in Attitude, if not in Expression. I dare say you have seen the Cast itself. And now for a Story better than either Print: a story to which Mrs. Siddons' glorious name leads me, burlesque as it is.

You may know there is a French Opera of Macbeth—by Chélard. This was being played at the Dublin Theatre—Viardot, I think, the Heroine.

However that may be, the Curtain drew up for the Sleep-walking Scene; Doctor and Nurse were there, while a long mysterious Symphony went on—till a Voice from the Gallery called out to the Leader of the Band, Levey—'Whisht! Lavy, my dear—tell us now—is it a Boy or a Girl?' This Story is in a Book which I gave 2*s.* for at a Railway Stall; called Recollections of an Impresario, or some such name; [82a] a Book you would not have deigned to read, and so would have missed what I have read and remembered and written out for you.

It will form the main part of my Letter: and surely you will not expect anything better from me.

Your hot Colorado Summer is over; and you are now coming to the season which you—and others beside you—think so peculiarly beautiful in America. We have no such Colours to show here, you know: none of that Violet which I think you have told me of as mixing with the Gold in the Foliage. Now it is that I hear that Spirit that Tennyson once told of talking to himself among the faded flowers in the Garden-plots. I think he has dropt that little Poem [82b] out of his acknowledged works; there was indeed nothing in it, I think, but that one Image: and that sticks by me as *Queen Mary* does not.

I have just been telling some Man enquiring in Notes and Queries where he may find the beautiful foolish old Pastoral beginning—

'My Sheep I neglected, I broke my Sheep-hook, &c.' [82c]

which, if you don't know it, I will write out for you, ready as it offers itself to my Memory. Mrs. Frere of Cambridge used to sing it as she could sing the Classical Ballad—to a fairly expressive tune: but there is a movement (Trio, I think) in one of dear old Haydn's Symphonies almost made for it. Who else but Haydn for the Pastoral! Do you remember his blessed Chorus of 'Come, gentle Spring,' that open the Seasons? Oh, it is something to remember the old Ladies who sang that Chorus at the old Ancient Concerts rising with Music in hand to sing that lovely piece under old Greatorex's Direction. I have never heard Haydn and Handel so well as in those old Rooms with those old Performers, who still retained the Tradition of those old Masters. Now it is getting Midnight; but so mild—this October 4—that I am going to smoke one Pipe outdoors—with a little Brandy and water to keep the Dews off. I told you I had not been well all the Summer; I say I begin to 'smell the Ground,' [83] which you will think all Fancy. But I remain while above Ground

Yours sincerely
E. F.G.

XXXIII.

DEAR MRS. KEMBLE,

My last Letter asked you how and where I could get at your Papers; this is to say, I have got them, thanks to the perseverance of our Woodbridge Bookseller, who would not be put off by his London Agent, and has finally procured me the three Numbers [84] which contain your 'Gossip.' Now believe me; I am delighted with it; and only wish it might run on as long as I live: which perhaps it may. Of course somewhat of my Interest results from the Times, Persons, and Places you write of; almost all more or less familiar to me; but I am quite sure that very few could have brought all before me as you have done—with what the Painters call, so free, full, and flowing a touch. I suppose this 'Gossip' is the Memoir you told me you were about; three or four years ago, I think: or perhaps Selections from it; though I hardly see how your Recollections could be fuller. No doubt your Papers will all be collected into a Book; perhaps it would have been financially better for you to have so published it now. But, on the other hand, you will have the advantage of writing with more freedom and ease in the Magazine, knowing that you can alter, contract, or amplify, in any future Re-publication. It gives me such pleasure to like, and honestly say I like, this work—and—I know I'm right in such matters, though I can't always give the reason why I like, or don't like, Dr. Fell: as much wiser People can—who reason themselves quite wrong.

I suppose you were at School in the Rue d'Angoulême near about the time (you don't give dates enough, I think—there's one fault for you!)—about the time when we lived there: I suppose you were somewhat later, however: for assuredly my Mother and yours would have been together often—Oh, but your Mother was not there, only you—at School. We were there in 1817-18—signalised by The Great Murder—that of Fualdès—one of the most interesting events in all History to me, I am sorry to say. For in that point I do not say I am right. But that Rue d'Angoulême—do you not remember the house cornering on the Champs Elysées with some ornaments in stone of Flowers and Garlands—belonging to a Lord Courtenay, I believe? And do you remember a Pépinière over the way; and, over that, seeing that Temple in the Beaujon Gardens with the Parisians descending and ascending in Cars? And (I think) at the end of the street, the Church of St. Philippe du Roule? Perhaps I shall see in your next Number that you do remember all these things.

Well: I was pleased with some other Papers in your Magazine: as those on V. Hugo, [85a] and Tennyson's Queen Mary: [85b] I doubt not that Criticism on English Writers is likely to be more impartial over the Atlantic, and not biassed by Clubs, Coteries, etc. I always say that we in the Country are safer Judges than those of even better Wits in London: not being prejudiced so much, whether by personal acquaintance, or party, or Fashion. I see that Professor Wilson said much the same thing to Willis forty years ago.

I have written to Donne to tell him of your Papers, and that I will send him my Copies if he cannot get them. Mowbray wrote me word that his Father, who has bought the house in Weymouth Street, was now about returning to it, after some Alterations made. Mowbray talks of paying me a little Visit here—he and his Wife—at the End of this month:—when what Good Looks we have will all be gone.

Farewell for the present; I count on your Gossip: and believe me (what it serves to make me feel more vividly)

Your sincere old Friend
E. F.G.

XXXIV.

[Nov. 1875.]

DEAR MRS. KEMBLE,

The Mowbray Donnes have been staying some days [86] with me—very pleasantly. Of course I got them to tell me of the fine things in London: among the rest, the Artists whose Photos they sent me, and I here enclose. The Lady, they tell me—(Spedding's present Idol)—is better than her Portrait—which would not have so enamoured Bassanio. Irving's, they say, is flattered. But 'tis a handsome face, surely; and one that should do for Hamlet—if it were not for that large Ear—do you notice? I was tempted to send it to you, because it reminds me of some of your Family: your Father, most of all, as Harlowe has painted him in that famous Picture of the Trial Scene. [87a] It is odd to me that the fine Engraving from that Picture—once so frequent—is scarce seen now: it has seemed strange to me to meet People who never even heard of it.

I don't know why you have a little Grudge against Mrs. Siddons—perhaps you will say you have not—all my fancy. I think it was noticed at Cambridge that your Brother John scarce went to visit her when she was staying with that Mrs. Frere, whom you don't remember with pleasure. She did talk much and loud: but she had a fine Woman's heart underneath, and she could sing a classical Song: as also some of Handel, whom she had

- 44 -

studied with Bartleman. But she never could have sung the Ballad with the fulness which you describe in Mrs. Arkwright. [87b]

Which, together with your mention of your American isolation, reminds me of some Verses of Hood, with which I will break your Heart a little. They are not so very good, neither: but I, in England as I am, and like to be, cannot forget them.

> 'The Swallow with Summer
>   Shall wing o'er the Seas;
> The Wind that I sigh to
>   Shall sing in your Trees;
>
> The Ship that it hastens
>   Your Ports will contain—
> But for me—I shall never
>   See England again.' [88a]

It always runs in my head to a little German Air, common enough in our younger days—which I will make a note of, and you will, I dare say, remember at once.

I doubt that what I have written is almost as illegible as that famous one of yours: in which however only [paper] was in fault: [88b] and now I shall scarce mend the matter by taking a steel pen instead of that old quill, which certainly did fight upon its Stumps.

Well now—Professor Masson of Edinburgh has asked me to join him and seventy-nine others in celebrating Carlyle's eightieth Birthday on December 4—with the Presentation of a Gold Medal with Carlyle's own Effigy upon it, and a congratulatory Address. I should have thought such a Measure would be ridiculous to Carlyle; but I suppose Masson must have ascertained his Pleasure from some intimate Friend of C.'s: otherwise he would not have known of my Existence for one. However Spedding and Pollock tell me that, after some hesitation like my own, they judged best to consent. Our Names are even to be attached somehow to a—White Silk, or Satin, Scroll! Surely Carlyle cannot be aware of that? I hope devoutly that my Name come too late for its Satin Apotheosis; but, if it do not, I shall apologise to Carlyle for joining such Mummery. I only followed the Example of my Betters.

Now I must shut up, for Photos and a Line of Music is to come in. I was so comforted to find that your Mother had some hand in Dr. Kitchener's Cookery Book, [89] which has always been Guide, Philosopher, and Friend in such matters. I can't help liking a Cookery Book.

Ever yours
E. F.G.

No: I never turned my tragic hand on Fualdès; but I remember well being taken in 1818 to the Ambigu Comique to see the 'Château de Paluzzi,' which was said to be founded on that great Murder. I still distinctly remember a Closet, from which came some guilty Personage. It is not only the Murder itself that impressed me, but the Scene it was enacted in; the ancient half-Spanish City of Rodez, with its River Aveyron, its lonely Boulevards, its great Cathedral, under which the Deed was done in the 'Rue des Hebdomadiers.' I suppose you don't see, or read, our present Whitechapel Murder—a nasty thing, not at all to my liking. The Name of the Murderer—as no one doubts he is, whatever the Lawyers may disprove—is the same as that famous Man of Taste who wrote on the Fine Arts in the London Magazine under the name of Janus Weathercock, [90a] and poisoned Wife, Wife's Mother and Sister after insuring their Lives.

De Quincey (who was one of the Magazine) has one of his Essays about this wretch.

Here is another half-sheet filled, after all: I am afraid rather troublesome to read. In three or four days we shall have another Atlantic, and I am ever yours

E. F.G.

XXXV.

WOODBRIDGE: *Dec*. 29/75.

DEAR MRS. KEMBLE,

You will say I am a very good Creature indeed, for beginning to answer your Letter the very day it reaches me. But so it happens that this same day also comes a Letter from Laurence the Painter, who tells me something of poor Minnie's Death, [90b] which answers to the Query in your Letter. Laurence sends me Mrs. Brookfield's Note to him: from which I quote to you—no!—I will make bold to send you her Letter itself! Laurence says he is generally averse to showing others a Letter meant for himself (the little Gentleman that he is!), but he ventures in this case, knowing me to be an old friend of the Family. And so I venture to post it over the Atlantic to you who take a sincere Interest in them also. I wonder if I am doing wrong?

In the midst of all this mourning comes out a new Volume of Thackeray's Drawings—or Sketches—as I foresaw it would be, too much Caricature, not so good as much [of] his old Punch; and with none of the better things

I wanted them to put in—for his sake, as well as the Community's. I do not wonder at the Publisher's obstinacy, but I wonder that Annie T. did not direct otherwise. I am convinced I can hear Thackeray saying, when such a Book as this was proposed to him—'Oh, come—there has been enough of all this'—and crumpling up the Proof in that little hand of his. For a curiously little hand he had, uncharacteristic of the grasp of his mind: I used to consider it half inherited from the Hindoo people among whom he was born. [91]

I dare say I told you of the Proposal to congratulate Carlyle on his eightieth Birthday; and probably some Newspaper has told you of the Address, and the Medal, and the White Satin Roll to which our eighty names were to be attached. I thought the whole Concern, Medal, Address, and Satin Roll, a very Cockney thing; and devoutly hoped my own illustrious name would arrive too late. I could not believe that Carlyle would like the Thing: but it appears by his published Answer that he did. He would not, ten years ago, I think. Now—talking of illustrious names, etc., oh, my dear Mrs. Kemble, your sincere old Regard for my Family and myself has made you say more—of one of us, at least—than the World will care to be told: even if your old Regard had not magnified our lawful Deserts. But indeed it has done so: in Quality, as well as in Quantity. I know I am not either squeamishly, or hypocritically, saying all this: I am sure I know myself better than you do, and take a juster view of my pretensions. I think you Kembles are almost Donnes in your determined regard, and (one may say) Devotion to old Friends, etc. A rare—a noble—Failing! Oh, dear!—Well, I shall not say any more: you will know that I do not the less thank you for publickly speaking of [me] as I never was spoken of before—only *too* well. Indeed, this is so; and when you come to make a Book of your Papers, I shall make you cut out something. Don't be angry with me now—no, I know you will not. [92]

The Day after To-morrow I shall have your new Number; which is a Consolation (if needed) for the Month's going. And I am ever yours

E. F.G.

Oh, I must add—The Printing is no doubt the more legible; but I get on very well with your MS. when not crossed. [94]

Donne, I hear, is fairly well. Mowbray has had a Lift in his Inland Revenue Office, and now is secure, I believe, of Competence for Life. Charles wrote me a kindly Letter at Christmas: he sent me his own Photo; and then (at my Desire) one of his wife:—Both of which I would enclose, but that my Packet is already bulky enough. It won't go off to-night when it is written—for here (absolutely!) comes my Reader (8 p.m.) to read me a

Story (very clever) in All the Year Round, and no one to go to Post just now.

Were they not pretty Verses by Hood? I thought to make you a little miserable by them:—but you take no more notice than—what you will.

Good Night! Good Bye!—Now for Mrs. Trollope's Story, entitled 'A Charming Fellow'—(very clever).

XXXVI.

WOODBRIDGE: *Febr.* 2/76.

Now, my dear Mrs. Kemble, I have done you a little good turn. Some days ago I was talking to my Brother John (I dared not show him!) of what you had said of my Family in your Gossip. He was extremely interested: and wished much that I [would] convey you his old hereditary remembrances. But, beside that, he wished you to have a Miniature of your Mother which my Mother had till she died. It is a full length; in a white Dress, with blue Scarf, looking and tending with extended Arms upward in a Blaze of Light. My Brother had heard my Mother's History of the Picture, but could not recall it. I fancy it was before your Mother's Marriage. The Figure is very beautiful, and the Face also: like your Sister Adelaide, and your Brother Henry both. I think you will be pleased with this: and my Brother is very pleased that you should have it. Now, how to get it over to you is the Question; I believe I must get my little Quaritch, the Bookseller, who has a great American connection, to get it safely over to you. But if you know of any surer means, let me know. It is framed: and would look much better if some black edging were streaked into the Gold Frame; a thing I sometimes do only with a strip of Black Paper. The old Plan of Black and Gold Frames is much wanted where Yellow predominates in the Picture. Do you know I have a sort of Genius for Picture-framing, which is an Art People may despise, as they do the Milliner's: but you know how the prettiest Face may be hurt, and the plainest improved, by the Bonnet; and I find that (like the Bonnet, I suppose) you can only judge of the Frame, by trying it on. I used to tell some Picture Dealers they had better hire me for such Millinery: but I have not had much Scope for my Art down here. So now you have a little Lecture along with the Picture.

Now, as you are to thank me for this good turn done to you, so have I to thank you for Ditto to me. The mention of my little Quaritch reminds me. He asked me for copies of Agamemnon, to give to some of his American Customers who asked for them; and I know from whom they must have somehow heard of it. And now, what Copies I had being gone, he is going, at his own risk, to publish a little Edition. The worst is, he *will* print it pretentiously, I fear, as if one thought it very precious: but the Truth is, I suppose he calculates on a few Buyers who will give what will repay him. One of my Patrons, Professor Norton, of Cambridge Mass., has sent me a second Series of Lowell's 'Among my Books,' which I shall be able to acknowledge with sincere praise. I had myself bought the first Series. Lowell may do for English Writers something as Ste. Beuve has done for French: and one cannot give higher Praise. [97a]

There has been an absurd Bout in the Athenæum [97b] between Miss Glyn and some Drury Lane Authorities. She wrote a Letter to say that she would not have played Cleopatra in a revival of Antony and Cleopatra for £1000 a line, I believe, so curtailed and mangled was it. Then comes a Miss Wallis, who played the Part, to declare that 'the Veteran' (Miss G.) had wished to play the Part as it was acted: and furthermore comes Mr. Halliday, who somehow manages and adapts at D. L., to assert that the Veteran not only wished to enact the Desecration, but did enact it for many nights when Miss Wallis was indisposed. Then comes Isabel forward again—but I really forget what she said. I never saw her but once—in the Duchess of Malfi— very well: better, I dare say, than anybody now; but one could not remember a Word, a Look, or an Action. She speaks in her Letter of being brought up in the grand School and Tradition of the Kembles.

I am glad, somehow, that you liked Macready's Reminiscences: so honest, so gentlemanly in the main, so pathetic even in his struggles to be a better Man and Actor. You, I think, feel with him in your Distaste for the Profession.

I write you tremendous long Letters, which you can please yourself about reading through. I shall write Laurence your message of Remembrance to him. I had a longish Letter from Donne, who spoke of himself as well enough, only living by strict Rule in Diet, Exercise, etc.

We have had some remarkable Alternations of Cold and Hot here too: but nothing like the extremes you tell me of on the other side of the Page.

Lionel Tennyson (second Son), who answered my half-yearly Letter to his father, tells me they had heard that Annie Thackeray was well in health, but—as you may imagine in Spirits.

And I remain yours always
E. F.G.

How is it my Atlantic Monthly is not yet come?

XXXVII.

WOODBRIDGE: *Febr.* 17/76.

DEAR MRS. KEMBLE,

I ought to have written before to apprise you of your Mother's Miniature being sent off—by Post. On consideration, we judged that to be the safest and speediest way: the Post Office here telling us that it was not too large or heavy so to travel: without the Frame. As, however, our Woodbridge Post Office is not very well-informed, I shall be very glad to hear it has reached you, in its double case: wood within, and tin without (quite unordered and unnecessary), which must make you think you receive a present of Sardines. You lose, you see, the Benefit of my exalted Taste in respect of Framing, which I had settled to perfection. Pray get a small Frame, concaving inwardly (Ogee pattern, I believe), which leads the Eyes into the Picture: whereas a Frame convexing outwardly leads the Eye away from the Picture; a very good thing in many cases, but not needed in this. I dare say the Picture (faded as it is) will look poor to you till enclosed and set off by a proper Frame. And the way is, as with a Bonnet (on which you know much depends even with the fairest face), to try one on before ordering it home. That is, if you choose to indulge in some more ornamental Frame than the quite simple one I have before named. Indeed, I am not sure if the Picture would not look best in a plain gold Flat (as it is called) without Ogee, or any ornament whatsoever. But try it on first: and then you can at least please yourself, if not the Terrible Modiste who now writes to you. My Brother is very anxious you should have the Picture, and wrote to me again to send you his hereditary kind Regards. I ought to be sending you his Note—which I have lost. Instead of that, I enclose one from poor Laurence to whom I wrote your kind message; and am as ever

Yours
E. F.G.

You will let me know if the Picture has not arrived before this Note reaches you?

XXXVIII.

LOWESTOFT: *March* 16/76.

DEAR MRS. KEMBLE,

Directly that you mentioned 'Urania,' I began to fancy I remembered her too. [100] And we are both right; I wrote to a London friend to look out for the Engraving: and I post it to you along with this Letter. If it do not reach you in some three weeks, let me know, and I will send another.

The Engraving stops short before the Feet: the Features are coarser than the Painting: which makes me suppose that it (Engraving) is from the

Painting: or from some Painting of which yours is a Copy—(I am called off here to see the Procession of Batty's Circus parade up the street)—

The Procession is past: the Clowns, the Fine Ladies (who should wear a little Rouge even by Daylight), the 'performing' Elephants, the helmeted Cavaliers, and last, the Owner (I suppose) as 'the modern Gentleman' driving four-in-hand.

This intoxication over, I return to my Duties—to say that the Engraving is from a Painting by 'P. Jean,' engraved by Vendramini: published by John Thompson in 1802, and dedicated to the 'Hon. W. R. Spencer'—(who, I suppose, was the 'Vers-de Société' Man of the Day; and perhaps the owner of the original: whether now yours, or not. All this I tell you in case the Print should not arrive in fair time: and you have but to let me know, and another shall post after it.

I have duly written my Brother your thanks for his Present, and your sincere Gratification in possessing it. He is very glad it has so much pleased you. But he can only surmise thus much more of its history—that it belonged to my Grandfather before my Mother: he being a great lover of the Theatre, and going every night I believe to old Covent Garden or old Drury Lane—names really musical to me—old Melodies.

I think I wrote to you about the Framing. I always say of that, as of other Millinery (on which so much depends), the best way is—to try on the Bonnet before ordering it; which you can do by the materials which all Carvers and Gilders in this Country keep by them. I have found even my Judgment—the Great Twalmley's Judgment—sometimes thrown out by not condescending to this; in this, as in so many other things, so very little making all the Difference. I should not think that Black next the Picture would do so well: but try, try: try on the Bonnet: and if you please yourself—inferior Modiste as you are—why, so far so good.

Donne, who reports himself as very well (always living by Discipline and Rule), tells me that he has begged you to return to England if you would make sure of seeing him again. I told Pollock of your great Interest in Macready: I too find that I am content to have bought the Book, and feel more interest in the Man than in the Actor. My Mother used to know him once: but I never saw him in private till once at Pollock's after his retirement: when he sat quite quiet, and (as you say) I was sorry not to have made a little Advance to him, as I heard he had a little wished to see me because of that old Acquaintance with my Mother. I should like to have told him how much I liked much of his Performance; asked him why he would say 'Amen stu-u-u-u-ck in my Throat' (which was a bit of wrong, as well as vulgar, Judgment, I think). But I looked on him as the great Man of the Evening, unpresuming as he was: and so kept aloof, as I have ever done from all Celebrities—yourself among them—who I thought must be wearied enough of Followers and Devotees—unless those of Note.

I am now writing in the place—in the room—from which I wrote ten years ago—it all recurs to me—with Montaigne for my Company, and my Lugger about to be built. Now I have brought Madame de Sévigné (who loved Montaigne too—the capital Woman!) and the Lugger—Ah, there is a long sad Story about that!—which I won't go into—

Little Quaritch seems to have dropt Agamemnon, Lord of Hosts, for the present: and I certainly am not sorry, for I think it would only have been abused by English Critics: with some, but not all, Justice. You are very good in naming your American Publisher, but I suppose it must be left at present with Quaritch, to whom I wrote a 'Permit,' so long as I had nothing to do with it.

Ever yours
E. F.G.

XXXIX.

[LOWESTOFT, *April*, 1876.]

MY DEAR MRS. KEMBLE,

From Lowestoft still I date: as just ten years ago when I was about building a Lugger, and reading Montaigne. The latter holds his own with me after three hundred years: and the Lugger does not seem much the worse for her ten years' wear, so well did she come bouncing between the Piers here yesterday, under a strong Sou'-Wester. My Great Captain has her no more; he has what they call a 'Scotch Keel' which is come into fashion: her too I see: and him too steering her, broader and taller than all the rest: fit to be a Leader of Men, Body and Soul; looking now Ulysses-like. Two or three years ago he had a run of constant bad luck; and, being always of a grand convivial turn, treating Everybody, he got deep in Drink, against all his Promises to me, and altogether so lawless, that I brought things to a pass between us. 'He should go on with me if he would take the Tee-total Pledge for one year'—'No—he had broken his word,' he said, 'and he would not pledge it again,' much as he wished to go on with me. That, you see, was very fine in him; he is altogether fine—A Great Man, I maintain it: like one of Carlyle's old Norway Kings, with a wider morality than we use; which is very good and fine (as this Captain said to me) 'for you who are born with a silver spoon in your mouths.' I did not forget what Carlyle too says about Great Faults in Great Men: even in David, the Lord's Anointed. But I thought best to share the Property with him and let him go his way. He had always resented being under any Control, and was very glad to be his own sole Master again: and yet clung to me in a wild and pathetic way. He has not been doing better since: and I fear is sinking into disorder.

This is a long story about one you know nothing about except what little I have told you. But the Man is a very remarkable Man indeed, and you may be interested—you must be—in him.

'Ho! parlons d'autres choses, ma Fille,' as my dear Sévigné says. She now occupies Montaigne's place in my room: well—worthily: she herself a Lover of Montaigne, and with a spice of his free thought and speech in her. I am sometimes vext I never made her acquaintance till last year: but perhaps it was as well to have such an acquaintance reserved for one's latter years. The fine Creature! much more alive to me than most Friends—I *should* like to see her 'Rochers' in Brittany. [105]

'Parlons d'autres choses'—your Mother's Miniature. You seemed at first to think it was taken from the Engraving: but the reverse was always clear to me. The whole figure, down to the Feet, is wanted to account for the position of the Legs; and the superior delicacy of Feature would not be gained *from* the Engraving, but the contrary. The Stars were stuck in to make an 'Urania' of it perhaps. I do not assert that your Miniature is the original: but that such a Miniature is. I did not expect that Black next the Picture would do: had you 'tried on the Bonnet' first, as I advised? I now wish I had sent the Picture over in its original Frame, which I had doctored quite well with a strip of Black Paper pasted over the Gold. It might really have gone through Quaritch's Agency: but I got into my head that the Post was safer. (How badly I am writing!) I had a little common Engraving of the Cottage bonnet Portrait: so like Henry. If I did not send it to you, I know not what is become of it.

Along with your Letter came one from Donne telling me of your Niece's Death. [106] He said he had written to tell you. In reply, I gave him your message; that he must 'hold on' till next year when peradventure you may see England again, and hope to see him too.

Sooner or later you will see an Account of 'Mary Tudor' at the Lyceum. [107] It is just what I expected: a 'succès d'estime,' and not a very enthusiastic one. Surely, no one could have expected more. And now comes out a new Italian Hamlet—Rossi—whose first appearance is recorded in the enclosed scrap of *Standard*. And (to finish Theatrical or Dramatic Business) Quaritch has begun to print Agamemnon—so leisurely that I fancy he wishes to wait till the old Persian is exhausted, and so join the two. I certainly am in no hurry; for I fully believe we shall only get abused for the Greek in proportion as we were praised for the Persian—in England. I mean: for you have made America more favourable.

'Parlons d'autres choses.' 'Eh? mais de quoi parler,' etc. Well: a Blackbird is singing in the little Garden outside my Lodging Window, which is frankly opened to what Sun there is. It has been a singular half year; only yesterday Thunder in rather cold weather; and last week the Road and Rail in Cambridge and Huntingdon was blocked up with Snow; and Thunder then also. I suppose I shall get home in ten days: before this Letter will reach you, I suppose: so your next may be addressed to Woodbridge. I really don't know if these long Letters are more of Trouble or Pleasure to you: however, there is an end to all: and that End is that I am yours as truly as ever I was

E. F.G.

XL.

WOODBRIDGE, *July* 4, [1876.]

DEAR MRS. KEMBLE,

Here I am back into the Country, as I may call my suburb here as compared to Lowestoft; all my house, except the one room—which 'serves me for Parlour and Bedroom and all' [108a]—occupied by Nieces. Our weather is temperate, our Trees green, Roses about to bloom, Birds about to leave off singing—all sufficiently pleasant. I must not forget a Box from Mudie with some Memoirs in it—of Godwin, Haydon, etc., which help to amuse one. And I am just beginning Don Quixote once more for my 'pièce de Résistance,' not being so familiar with the First Part as the Second. Lamb and Coleridge (I think) thought that Second Part should not have been written; why then did I—not for contradiction's sake, I am sure—so much prefer it? Old Hallam, in his History of Literature, resolved me, I believe, by saying that Cervantes, who began by making his Hero ludicrously crazy, fell in love with him, and in the second part tamed and tempered him down to the grand Gentleman he is: scarce ever originating a Delusion, though acting his part in it as a true Knight when led into it by others. [108b] A good deal however might well be left out. If you have Jarvis' Translation by, or near, you, pray read—oh, read all of the second part, except the stupid stuff of the old Duenna in the Duke's Palace.

I fear I get more and more interested in your 'Gossip,' as you approach the Theatre. I suppose indeed that it is better to look on than to be engaged in. I love it, and reading of it, now as much as ever I cared to see it: and that was, very much indeed. I never heard till from your last Paper [109a] that Henry was ever thought of for Romeo: I wonder he did not tell me this when he and I were in Paris in 1830, and used to go and see 'La Muette!' (I can hear them calling it now:) at the Grand Opera. I see that

- 54 -

'Queen Mary' has some while since been deposed from the Lyceum; and poor Mr. Irving descended from Shakespeare to his old Melodrama again. All this is still interesting to me down here: much more than to you—over there!—

'Over there' you are in the thick of your Philadelphian Exhibition, [109b] I suppose: but I dare say you do not meddle with it very much, and will probably be glad when it is all over. I wish now I had sent you the Miniature in its Frame, which I had instructed to become it. What you tell us your Mother said concerning Dress, I certainly always felt: only secure the Beautiful, and the Grand, in all the Arts, whatever Chronology may say. Rousseau somewhere says that what you want of Decoration in the Theatre is, what will bewilder the Imagination—'ébranler l'Imagination,' I think: [110] only let it be Beautiful!

June 5.

I kept this letter open in case I should see Arthur Malkin, who was coming to stay at a Neighbour's house. He very kindly did call on me: he and his second wife (who, my Neighbour says, is a very proper Wife), but I was abroad—though no further off than my own little Estate; and he knows I do not visit elsewhere. But I do not the less thank him, and am always yours

E. F.G.

Pollock writes me he had just visited Carlyle—quite well for his Age: and vehement against Darwin, and the Turk.

XLI.

WOODBRIDGE, *July* 31/76.

DEAR MRS. KEMBLE,

A better pen than usual tempts me to write the little I have to tell you; so that [at] any rate your Eyes shall not be afflicted as sometimes I doubt they are by my MS.

Which MS. puts me at once in mind of Print: and to tell you that I shall send you Quaritch's Reprint of Agamemnon: which is just done after many blunders. The revises were not sent me, as I desired: so several things are left as I meant not: but 'enfin' here it is at last so fine that I am ashamed of it. For, whatever the merit of it may be, it can't come near all this fine Paper, Margin, etc., which Quaritch *will* have as counting on only a few buyers, who will buy—in America almost wholly, I think. And, as this is wholly due to you, I send you the Reprint, however little different to what you had before.

'Tragedy wonders at being so fine,' which leads me to that which ought more properly to have led to *it*: your last two Papers of 'Gossip,' which are capital, both for the Story told, and the remarks that arise from it. To-morrow, or next day, I shall have a new Number; and I really do count rather childishly on their arrival. Spedding also is going over some of his old Bacon ground in the Contemporary, [111] and his writing is always delightful to me though I cannot agree with him at last. I am told he is in full Vigour: as indeed I might guess from his writing. I heard from Donne some three weeks ago: proposing a Summer Holyday at Whitby, in Yorkshire: Valentia, I think, not very well again: Blanche then with her Brother Charles. They all speak very highly of Mrs. Santley's kindness and care. Mowbray talks of coming down this way toward the end of August: but had not, when he last wrote, fixed on his Holyday place.

Beside my two yearly elder Nieces, I have now a younger who has spent the last five Winters in Florence with your once rather intimate (I think) Jane FitzGerald my Sister. She married, (you may know) a Clergyman considerably older than herself. I wrote to Annie Thackeray lately, and had an answer (from the Lakes) to say she was pretty well—as also Mr. Stephen.

And I am ever yours
E. F.G.

P.S. On second thoughts I venture to send you A. T.'s letter, which may interest you and cannot shame her. I do not want it again.

XLII.

WOODBRIDGE: *Sept*. 21/76.

DEAR MRS. KEMBLE,

Have your American Woods begun to hang out their Purple and Gold yet? on this Day of Equinox. Some of ours begin to look rusty, after the Summer Drought; but have not turned Yellow yet. I was talking of this to a Heroine of mine who lives near here, but visits the Highlands of Scotland, which she loves better than Suffolk—and she said of those Highland Trees—'O, they give themselves no dying Airs, but turn Orange in a Day, and are swept off in a Whirlwind, and Winter is come.'

Now too one's Garden begins to be haunted by that Spirit which Tennyson says is heard talking to himself among the flower-borders. Do you remember him? [113a]

And now—Who should send in his card to me last week—but the old Poet himself—he and his elder Son Hallam passing through Woodbridge from a Tour in Norfolk. [113b] 'Dear old Fitz,' ran the Card in pencil, 'We are passing thro'.' [113c] I had not seen him for twenty years—he looked much the same, except for his fallen Locks; and what really surprised me was, that we fell at once into the old Humour, as if we had only been parted twenty Days instead of so many Years. I suppose this is a Sign of Age—not altogether desirable. But so it was. He stayed two Days, and we went over the same old grounds of Debate, told some of the old Stories, and all was well. I suppose I may never see him again: and so I suppose we both thought as the Rail carried him off: and each returned to his ways as if scarcely diverted from them. Age again!—I liked Hallam much; unaffected, unpretending—no Slang—none of Young England's nonchalance— speaking of his Father as 'Papa' and tending him with great Care, Love, and Discretion. Mrs. A. T. is much out of health, and scarce leaves Home, I think. [114a]

I have lately finished Don Quixote again, and I think have inflamed A. T. to read him too—I mean in his native Language. For this *must* be, good as Jarvis' Translation is, and the matter of the Book so good that one would think it would lose less than any Book by Translation. But somehow that is not so. I was astonished lately to see how Shakespeare's Henry IV. came out in young V. Hugo's Prose Translation [114b]: Hotspur, Falstaff and all. It really seemed to show me more than I had yet seen in the original.

Ever yours,
E. F.G.

XLIII.

LOWESTOFT: *October* 24/76.

DEAR MRS. KEMBLE,

Little—Nothing—as I have to write, I am nevertheless beginning to write to you, from this old Lodging of mine, from which I think our Correspondence chiefly began—ten years ago. I am in the same Room: the same dull Sea moaning before me: the same Wind screaming through the Windows: so I take up the same old Story. My Lugger was then about building: [115] she has passed into other hands now: I see her from time to time bouncing into Harbour, with her '244' on her Bows. Her Captain and I have parted: I thought he did very wrongly—Drink, among other things: but he did not think he did wrong: a different Morality from ours—that, indeed, of Carlyle's ancient Sea Kings. I saw him a few days ago in his house, with Wife and Children; looking, as always, too big for his house:

but always grand, polite, and unlike anybody else. I was noticing the many Flies in the room—'Poor things,' he said, 'it is the warmth of our Stove makes them alive.' When Tennyson was with me, whose Portrait hangs in my house in company with those of Thackeray and this Man (the three greatest men I have known), I thought that both Tennyson and Thackeray were inferior to him in respect of Thinking of Themselves. When Tennyson was telling me of how The Quarterly abused him (humorously too), and desirous of knowing why one did not care for his later works, etc., I thought that if he had lived an active Life, as Scott and Shakespeare; or even ridden, shot, drunk, and played the Devil, as Byron, he would have done much more, and talked about it much less. 'You know,' said Scott to Lockhart, 'that I don't care a Curse about what I write,' [116] and one sees he did not. I don't believe it was far otherwise with Shakespeare. Even old Wordsworth, wrapt up in his Mountain mists, and proud as he was, was above all this vain Disquietude: proud, not vain, was he: and that a Great Man (as Dante) has some right to be—but not to care what the Coteries say. What a Rigmarole!

Donne scarce ever writes to me (Twalmley the Great), and if he do not write to you, depend upon it he thinks he has nothing worth sending over the Atlantic. I heard from Mowbray quite lately that his Father was very well.

Yes: you told me in a previous Letter that you were coming to England after Christmas. I shall not be up to going to London to see you, with all your Company about you; perhaps (don't think me very impudent!) you may come down, if we live till Summer, to my Woodbridge Château, and there talk over some old things.

I make a kind of Summer in my Room here with Boccaccio. What a Mercy that one can return with a Relish to these Books! As Don Quixote can only be read in his Spanish, so I do fancy Boccaccio only in his Italian: and yet one is used to fancy that Poetry is the mainly untranslateable thing. How prettily innocent are the Ladies, who, after telling very loose Stories, finish with 'E così Iddio faccia [noi] godere del nostro Amore, etc.,' sometimes, *Domeneddio*, more affectionately. [117a]

Anyhow, these Ladies are better than the accursed Eastern Question; [117b] of which I have determined to read, and, if possible, hear, no more till the one question be settled of Peace or War. If war, I am told I may lose some £5000 in Russian Bankruptcy: but I can truly say I would give that, and more, to ensure Peace and Good Will among Men at this time. Oh, the Apes we are! I must retire to my Montaigne—whom, by the way, I remember reading here, when the Lugger was building! Oh, the Apes, etc.

But there was A Man in all that Business still, who is so now, somewhat tarnished.—And I am yours as then sincerely

E. F.G.

XLIV.

LOWESTOFT: *December* 12/76.

DEAR MRS. KEMBLE,

If you hold to your Intention of coming to Europe in January, this will be my last Letter over the Atlantic—till further Notice! I dare say you will send me a last Rejoinder under the same conditions.

I write, you see, from the Date of my last letter: but have been at home in the meanwhile. And am going home to-morrow—to arrange about Christmas Turkeys (God send we haven't all our fill of that, this Year!) and other such little matters pertaining to the Season—which, to myself, is always a very dull one. Why it happens that I so often write to you from here, I scarce know; only that one comes with few Books, perhaps, and the Sea somehow talks to one of old Things. I have ever my Edition of Crabbe's Tales of the Hall with me. How pretty is this—

> 'In a small Cottage on the rising Ground
> West of the Waves, and just beyond their Sound.' [118]

Which reminds me also that one of the Books I have here is Leslie Stephen's 'Hours in a Library,' really delightful reading, and, I think, really settling some Questions of Criticism, as one wants to be finally done in all Cases, so as to have no more about and about it. I think I could have suggested a little Alteration in the matter of this Crabbe, whom I probably am better up in than L. S., though I certainly could not write about it as he does. Also, one word about *Clarissa*. Almost all the rest of the two Volumes I accept as a Disciple. [119a]

Another Book of the kind—Lowell's 'Among my Books,' is excellent also: perhaps with more *Genius* than Stephen: but on the other hand not so temperate, judicious, or scholarly in *taste*. It was Professor Norton who sent me Lowell's Second Series; and, if you should—(as you inevitably will, though in danger of losing the Ship) answer this Letter, pray tell me if you know how Professor Norton is—in health, I mean. You told me he was very delicate: and I am tempted to think he may be less well than usual, as he has not acknowledged the receipt of a Volume [119b] I sent him with some of Wordsworth's Letters in it, which he had wished to see. The Volume did not need Acknowledgment absolutely: but probably would not have been received without by so amiable and polite a Man, if he [were] not out of sorts. I should really be glad to hear that he has only forgotten, or neglected, to write.

Mr. Lowell's Ode [120a] in your last Magazine seemed to me full of fine Thought; but it wanted Wings. I mean it kept too much to one Level, though a high Level, for Lyric Poetry, as Ode is supposed to be: both in respect to Thought, and Metre. Even Wordsworth (least musical of men) changed his Flight to better purpose in his Ode to Immortality. Perhaps, however, Mr. Lowell's subject did not require, or admit, such Alternations.

Your last Gossip brought me back to London—but what Street I cannot make sure of—but one Room in whatever Street it were, where I remember your Mr. Wade, who took his Defeat at the Theatre so bravely. [120b] And your John, in Spain with the Archbishop of Dublin: and coming home full of Torrijos: and singing to me and Thackeray one day in Russell Street: [120c]

Si un E - li - o con - spi - ro a - le - vo - -
so contra el pueb - lo y su .. li - ber - tad .... &c.

All which comes to me west of the waves and just within the sound: and is to travel so much farther Westward over an Expanse of Rollers such as we see not in this Herring-pond. Still, it is—The Sea.

Now then Farewell, dear Mrs. Kemble. You will let me know when you get to Dublin? I will add that, after very many weeks, I did hear from Donne, who told me of you, and that he himself had been out to dine: and was none the worse.

And I still remain, you see, your long-winded Correspondent

E. F.G.

XLV.

12 MARINE TERRACE, LOWESTOFT,
February 19/77.

DEAR MRS. KEMBLE,

Donne has sent me the Address on the cover of this Letter. I know you will write directly you hear from me; that is 'de rigueur' with you; and, at any rate, you have your Voyage home to England to tell me of: and how you find yourself and all in the Old Country. I suppose you include my Old Ireland in it. Donne wrote that you were to be there till this Month's end; that is drawing near; and, if that you do not protract your Visit, you will [be] very soon within sight of dear Donne himself, who, I hear from Mowbray, is very well.

Your last Gossip was very interesting to me. I see in it (but not in the most interesting part) [122a] that you write of a 'J. F.,' who tells you of a Sister of hers having a fourth Child, etc. I fancy this must be a Jane FitzGerald telling you of her Sister Kerrich, who would have numbered about so many Children about that time—1831. Was it that Jane? I think you and she were rather together just then. After which she married herself to a Mr. Wilkinson—made him very Evangelical—and tiresome—and so they fed their Flock in a Suffolk village. [122b] And about fourteen or fifteen years ago he died: and she went off to live in Florence—rather a change from the Suffolk Village—and there, I suppose, she will die when her Time comes.

Now you have read Harold, I suppose; and you shall tell me what you think of it. Pollock and Miladi think it has plenty of Action and Life: one of which Qualities I rather missed in it.

Mr. Lowell sent me his Three Odes about Liberty, Washington, etc. They seemed to me full of fine Thought, and in a lofty Strain: but wanting Variety both of Mood and Diction for Odes—which are supposed to mean things to be chanted. So I ventured to hint to him—Is he an angry man? But he wouldn't care, knowing of me only through amiable Mr. Norton, who knows me through you. I think *he* must be a very amiable, modest, man. And I am still yours always

E. F.G.

XLVI.

12 MARINE TERRACE, LOWESTOFT,
March 15, [1877.

DEAR MRS. KEMBLE,

By this time you are, I suppose, at the Address you gave me, and which will now cover this Letter. You have seen Donne, and many Friends, perhaps—and perhaps you have not yet got to London at all. But you will in time. When you do, you will, I think, have your time more taken up than in America—with so many old Friends about you: so that I wish more and more you would not feel bound to answer my Letters, one by one; but I suppose you will.

What I liked so much in your February Atlantic [123] was all about Goethe and Portia: I think, *fine* writing, in the plain sense of the word, and partly so because not 'fine' in the other Sense. You can indeed spin out a long

Sentence of complicated Thought very easily, and very clearly; a rare thing. As to Goethe, I made another Trial at Hayward's Prose Translation this winter, but failed, as before, to get on with it. I suppose there is a Screw loose in me on that point, seeing what all thinking People think of it. I am sure I have honestly tried. As to Portia, I still think she ought not to have proved her 'Superiority' by withholding that simple Secret on which her Husband's Peace and his Friend's Life depended. Your final phrase about her 'sinking into perfection' is capital. Epigram—without Effort.

You wrote me that Portia was your *beau-ideal* of Womanhood [124a]—Query, of *Lady-hood*. For she had more than £500 a year, which Becky Sharp thinks enough to be very virtuous on, and had not been tried. Would she have done Jeanie Deans' work? She might, I believe: but was not tried.

I doubt all this will be rather a Bore to you: coming back to England to find all the old topics of Shakespeare, etc., much as you left them. You will hear wonderful things about Browning and Co.—Wagner—and H. Irving. In a late TEMPLE BAR magazine [124b] Lady Pollock says that her Idol Irving's Reading of Hood's Eugene Aram is such that any one among his Audience who had a guilty secret in his Bosom 'must either tell it, or die.' These are her words.

You see I still linger in this ugly place: having a very dear little Niece a little way off: a complete little 'Pocket-Muse' I call her. One of the first Things she remembers is—*you*, in white Satin, and very handsome, she says, reading Twelfth Night at this very place. And I am

Yours ever
E. F.G.

(I am now going to make out a Dictionary-list of the People in my dear Sévigné, for my own use.) [125a]

XLVII.

LITTLE GRANGE: WOODBRIDGE.
May 5/77.

DEAR MRS. KEMBLE,

I am disappointed at not finding any Gossip in the last Atlantic; [125b] the Editor told us at the end of last Year that it was to be carried on through this: perhaps you are not bound down to every month: but I hope the links are not to discontinue for long.

I did not mean in my last letter to allude again to myself and Co. in recommending some omissions when you republish. [126] That—*viz.*, about myself—I was satisfied you would cut out, as we had agreed before. (N.B. No occasion to omit your kindly Notices about my Family—nor my own Name among them, if you like: only not all about myself.) What I meant in my last Letter was, some of your earlier Letters—or parts of Letters—to H.—as some from Canterbury, I think—I fancy some part of your early Life might be condensed. But I will tell you, if you will allow me, when the time comes: and then you can but keep to your own plan, which you have good reason to think better than mine—though I am very strong in Scissors and Paste: my 'Harp and Lute.' Crabbe is under them now—as usual, once a Year. If one lived in London, or in any busy place, all this would not be perhaps: but it hurts nobody—unless you, who do hear too much about it.

Last night I made my Reader begin Dickens' wonderful 'Great Expectations': not considered one of his best, you know, but full of wonderful things, and even with a Plot which, I think, only needed less intricacy to be admirable. I had only just read the Book myself: but I wanted to see what my Reader would make of it: and he was so interested that he re-interested me too. Here is another piece of Woodbridge Life.

Now, if when London is hot you should like to run down to this Woodbridge, here will be my house at your Service after July. It may be so all this month: but a Nephew, Wife, and Babe did talk of a Fortnight's Visit: but have not talked of it since I returned a fortnight ago. June and July my Invalid Niece and her Sister occupy the House—not longer. Donne, and all who know me, know that I do not like anyone to come out of their way to visit me: but, if they be coming this way, I am very glad to do my best for them. And if any of them likes to occupy my house at any time, here it is at their Service—at yours, for as long as you will, except the times I have mentioned. I give up the house entirely except my one room, which serves for Parlour and Bed: and which I really prefer, as it reminds me of the Cabin of my dear little Ship—mine no more.

Here is a long Story about very little. Woodbridge again.

A Letter from Mowbray Donne told me that you had removed to some house in—Connaught Place? [127a]—but he did not name the number.

Valentia's wedding comes on: perhaps you will be of the Party. [127b] I think it would be one more of Sorrow than of Gladness to me: but perhaps that may be the case with most Bridals.

It is very cold here: ice of nights: but my Tulips and Anemones hold up still: and Nightingales sing. Somehow, I don't care for those latter at Night. They ought to be in Bed like the rest of us. This seems talking for the sake of being singular: but I have always felt it, singular or not.

And I am yours always

E. F.G.

XLVIII.

[*June*, 1877.]

MY DEAR MRS. KEMBLE,

I only write now on the express condition (which I understand you to accept) that you will not reply till you are in Switzerland. I mean, of course, within any reasonable time. Your last Letter is not a happy one *: but the record of your first Memoir cannot fail to interest and touch me.

I surmise—for you do not say so—that you are alone in London now: then, you must get away as soon as you can; and I shall be very glad to hear from yourself that you are in some green Swiss Valley, with a blue Lake before you, and snowy mountain above.

I must tell you that, my Nieces being here—good, pious, and tender, they are too—(but one of them an Invalid, and the other devoted to attend her) they make but little change in my own way of Life. They live by themselves, and I only see them now and then in the Garden—sometimes not five minutes in the Day. But then I am so long used to Solitude. And there is an end of that Chapter.

I have your Gossip bound up: the binder backed it with Black, which I don't like (it was his doing, not mine), but you say that your own only Suit is Sables now. I am going to lend it to a very admirable Lady who is going to our ugly Sea-side, with a sick Brother: only I have pasted over one column—*which*, I leave you to guess at.

I think I never told you—what is the fact, however—that I had wished to dedicate Agamemnon to you, but thought I could not do so without my own name appended. Whereas, I could, very simply, as I saw afterwards when too late. If ever he is reprinted I shall (unless you forbid) do as I desired to do: for, if for no other reason, he would probably never have been published but for you. Perhaps he had better [have] remained in private Life so far as England is concerned. And so much for that grand Chapter.

I think it is an ill-omened Year: beside War (which I *won't* read about) so much Illness and Death—hereabout, at any rate. A Nephew of mine—a capital fellow—was pitched upon his head from a Gig a week ago, and we know not yet how far that head of his may recover itself. But, beside one's own immediate Friends, I hear of Sickness and Death from further

Quarters; and our Church Bell has been everlastingly importunate with its "Toll-toll." But Farewell for the present: pray do as I ask you about writing: and believe me ever yours,

E. F.G.

* You were thinking of something else when you misdirected your letter, which sent it a round before reaching Woodbridge.

XLIX.

WOODBRIDGE, *June* 23/77.

DEAR MRS. KEMBLE,

I knew the best thing I could do concerning the Book you wanted was to send your Enquiry to the Oracle itself:—whose Reply I herewith enclose.

Last Evening I heard read Jeanie Deans' Audience with Argyle, and then with the Queen. There I stop with the Book. Oh, how refreshing is the leisurely, easy, movement of the Story, with its true, and well-harmonized Variety of Scene and Character! There is of course a Bore—Saddletree—as in Shakespeare. I presume to think—as in Cervantes—as in Life itself: somewhat too much of him in Scott, perhaps. But when the fuliginous and Spasmodic Carlyle and Co. talk of Scott's delineating his Characters from without to within [131a]—why, he seems to have had a pretty good Staple of the inner Man of David, and Jeanie Deans, on beginning his Story; as of the Antiquary, Dalgetty, the Ashtons, and a lot more. I leave all but the Scotch Novels. Madge has a little—a wee bit—theatrical about her: but I think her to be paired off with Ophelia, and worth all Miss Austen's Drawing-room Respectabilities put together. It is pretty what Barry Cornwall says on meeting Scott among other Authors at Rogers': 'I do not think any one envied him any more than one envies Kings.' [131b] You have done him honour in your Gossip: as one ought to do in these latter Days.

So this will be my last letter to you till you write me from Switzerland: where I wish you to be as soon as possible. And am yours always and sincerely

E. F.G.

A Letter from Donne speaks cheerfully. And Charles to be married again! It may be best for him.

L.

31, GREAT GEORGE STREET, S.W.
Feb. 20, 1878.

DEAR EDWARD FITZGERALD,

I have sent your book ('Mrs. Kemble's Autobiography') as far as Bealings by a safe convoy, and my cousin, Elizabeth Phillips, who is staying there, will ultimately convey it to its destination at your house.

It afforded Charlotte [wife] and myself several evenings of very agreeable reading, and we certainly were impressed most favourably with new views as to the qualities of heart and head of the writer. Some observations were far beyond what her years would have led one to expect. I think some letters to her friend 'S.' on the strange fancy which hurried off her brother from taking orders, to fighting Spanish quarrels, are very remarkable for their good sense, as well as warm feeling. Her energy too in accepting her profession at the age of twenty as a means of assisting her father to overcome his difficulties is indicative of the best form of genius—steady determination to an end.

Curiously enough, whilst reading the book, we met Mrs. Gordon (a daughter of Mrs. Sartoris) and her husband at Malkin's at dinner, and I had the pleasure of sitting next to her. The durability of type in the Kemble face might be a matter for observation with physiologists, and from the little I saw of her I should think the lady worthy of the family.

If the book be issued in a reprint a few omissions might be well. I fear we lost however by some lacunæ which you had caused by covering up a page or two.

Charlotte unites with me in kindest regards to yourself

Yours very sincerely,
HATHERLEY.

E. FITZGERALD, ESQ.

I send this to you, dear Mrs. Kemble, not because the writer is a Lord—Ex-Chancellor—but a very good, amiable, and judicious man. I should have sent you any other such testimony, had not all but this been oral, only this one took away the Book, and thus returns it. I had forgot to ask about the Book; oh, make Bentley do it; if any other English Publisher should meditate doing so, he surely will apprise you; and you can have some Voice in it.

Ever yours
E. F.G.

No need to return, or acknowledge, the Letter.

LI.

LITTLE GRANGE: WOODBRIDGE.
February 22, [1878.]

MY DEAR LADY,

I am calling on you earlier than usual, I think. In my 'Academy' [134a] I saw mention of some Notes on Mrs. Siddons in some article of this month's 'Fortnightly' [134b]—as I thought. So I bought the Number, but can find no Siddons there. You probably know about it; and will tell me?

If you have not already read—*buy* Keats' Love-Letters to Fanny Brawne. One wishes she had another name; and had left some other Likeness of herself than the Silhouette (cut out by Scissors, I fancy) which dashes one's notion of such a Poet's worship. But one knows what misrepresentations such Scissors make. I had—perhaps have—one of Alfred Tennyson, done by an Artist on a Steamboat—some thirty years ago; which, though not inaccurate of outline, gave one the idea of a respectable Apprentice. [134c] But Keats' Letters—It happened that, just before they reached me, I had been hammering out some admirable Notes on Catullus [135a]—another such fiery Soul who perished about thirty years of age two thousand years ago; and I scarce felt a change from one to other. [135b] From Catullus' better parts, I mean; for there is too much of filthy and odious—both of Love and Hate. Oh, my dear Virgil never fell into that: he was fit to be Dante's companion beyond even Purgatory.

I have just had a nice letter from Mr. Norton in America: an amiable, modest man surely he must be. His aged Mother has been ill: fallen indeed into some half-paralysis: affecting her Speech principally. He says nothing of Mr. Lowell; to whom I would write if I did not suppose he was very busy with his Diplomacy, and his Books, in Spain. I hope he will give us a Cervantes, in addition to the Studies in his 'Among my Books,' which seem to me, on the whole, the most conclusive Criticisms we have on their several subjects.

Do you ever see Mrs. Ritchie? Fred. Tennyson wrote me that Alfred's son (Lionel, the younger, I suppose) was to be married in Westminster Abbey: which Fred, thinks an ambitious flight of Mrs. A. T.

I may as well stop in such Gossip. Snowdrops and Crocuses out: I have not many, for what I had have been buried under an overcoat of Clay, poor little Souls. Thrushes tuning up; and I hope my old Blackbirds have not forsaken me, or fallen a prey to Cats.

And I am ever yours
E. F.G.

LII.

THE OLD (CURIOSITY) SHOP. WOODBRIDGE,
April 16, [1878.]

[Where, by the by, I heard the Nightingale for the first time yesterday Morning. That is, I believe, almost its exact date of return, wind and weather permitting. Which being premised—]

DEAR MRS. KEMBLE,

I think it is about the time for you to have a letter from me; for I think I am nearly as punctual as the Nightingale, though at quicker Intervals; and perhaps there may be other points of Unlikeness. After hearing that first Nightingale in my Garden, I found a long, kind, and pleasant, Letter from Mr. Lowell in Madrid: the first of him too that I have heard since he flew thither. Just before he wrote, he says, he had been assigning Damages to some American who complained of having been fed too long on Turtle's Eggs [136]:—and all that sort of Business, says the Minister, does not inspire a man to Letter-writing. He is acclimatizing himself to Cervantes, about whom he must write one of his fine, and (as I think) final Essays: I mean such as (in the case of others he has done) ought to leave no room for a reversal of Judgment. Amid the multitude of Essays, Reviews, etc., one still wants *that*: and I think Lowell does it more than any other Englishman. He says he meets Velasquez at every turn of the street; and Murillo's Santa Anna opens his door for him. Things are different here: but when my Oracle last night was reading to me of Dandie Dinmont's blessed visit to Bertram in Portanferry Gaol, I said—'I know it's Dandie, and I shouldn't be at all surprised to see him come into this room.' No—no more than— Madame de Sévigné! I suppose it is scarce right to live so among Shadows; but—after near seventy years so passed—'Que voulez-vous?'

Still, if any Reality would—of its own Volition—draw near to my still quite substantial Self; I say that my House (if the Spring do not prove unkindly) will be ready to receive—and the owner also—any time before June, and after July; that is, before Mrs. Kemble goes to the Mountains, and after she returns from them. I dare say no more, after so much so often said, and all about oneself.

Yesterday the Nightingale; and To-day a small, still, Rain which we had hoped for, to make 'poindre' the Flower-seeds we put in Earth last Saturday. All Sunday my white Pigeons were employed in confiscating the Sweet Peas we had laid there; so that To-day we have to sow the same anew.

I think a Memoir of Alfred de Musset, by his Brother, well worth reading. [138a] I don't say the best, but only to myself the most acceptable of modern French Poets; and, as I judge, a fine fellow—of the moral French type (I suppose some of the Shadow is left out of the Sketch), but of a Soul quite abhorrent from modern French Literature—from V. Hugo (I think) to E. Sue (I am sure). He loves to read—Clarissa! which reminded me of Tennyson, some forty years ago, saying to me *à propos* of that very book, 'I love those large, *still*, Books.' During a long Illness of A. de M. a Sister of the Bon Secours attended him: and, when she left, gave him a Pen worked in coloured Silks, 'Pensez à vos promesses,' as also a little 'amphore' she had knitted. Seventeen years (I think) after, when his last Illness came on him, he desired these two things to be enclosed in his Coffin. [138b]

And I am ever yours
E. F.G.

LIII.

DUNWICH: *August* 24, [1878.]

DEAR MRS. KEMBLE,

I forget if I wrote to you from this solitary Seaside, last year: telling you of its old Priory walls, etc. I think you must have been in Switzerland when I was here; however, I'll not tell you the little there is to tell about it now; for, beside that I may have told it all before, this little lodging furnishes only a steel pen, and very diluted ink (as you see), and so, for your own sake, I will be brief. Indeed, my chief object in writing at all, is, to ask when you go abroad, and how you have done at Malvern since last I heard from you— now a month ago, I think.

About the beginning of next week I shall be leaving this place—for good, I suppose—for the two friends—Man and Wife—who form my Company here, living a long musket shot off, go away—he in broken health—and would leave the place too solitary without them. So I suppose I shall decamp along with them; and, after some time spent at Lowestoft, find my way back to Woodbridge—in time to see the End of the Flowers, and to prepare what is to be done in that way for another Year.

And to Woodbridge your Answer may be directed, if this poor Letter of mine reaches you, and you should care to answer it—as you will—oh yes, you will—were it much less significant.

I have been rather at a loss for Books while here, Mudie having sent me a lot I did not care for—not even for Lady Chatterton. Aldis Wright gave me his Edition of Coriolanus to read; and I did not think '*pow wow*' of it, as Volumnia says. All the people were talking about me.

And I am ever yours truly
E. F.G.

LIV.

WOODBRIDGE: *April* 3/79.

MY DEAR MRS. KEMBLE:—

I know well how exact you are in answering Letters; and I was afraid that you must be in some trouble, for yourself, or others, when I got no reply to a second Letter I wrote you addressed to Baltimore Hotel, Leamington— oh, two months ago. When you last wrote to me, you were there, with a Cough, which you were just going to take with you to Guy's Cliff. That I thought not very prudent, in the weather we then had. Then I was told by some one, in a letter (not from any Donne, I think—no, Annie Ritchie, I believe) that Mrs. Sartoris was very ill; and so between two probable troubles, I would not trouble you as yet again. I had to go to London for a day three weeks ago (to see a poor fellow dying, sooner or later, of Brain disease), and I ferreted out Mowbray Donne from Somerset House and he told me you were in London, still ill of a Cough; but not your Address. So I wrote to his Wife a few days ago to learn it; and I shall address this Letter accordingly. Mrs. Mowbray writes that you are better, but obliged to take care of yourself. I can only say 'do not trouble yourself to write'—but I suppose you will—perhaps the more if it be a trouble. See what an Opinion I have of you!—If you write, pray tell me of Mrs. Sartoris—and do not forget yourself.

It has been such a mortal Winter among those I know, or know of, as I never remember. I have not suffered myself, further than, I think, feeling a few stronger hints of a constitutional sort, which are, I suppose, to assert themselves ever more till they do for me. And that, I suppose, cannot be long adoing. I entered on my 71st year last Monday, March 31.

My elder—and now only—Brother, John, has been shut up with Doctor and Nurse these two months—Æt. 76; his Wife Æt. 80 all but dead awhile ago, now sufficiently recovered to keep her room in tolerable ease: I do not know if my Brother will ever leave his house.

Oh dear! Here is enough of Mortality.

I see your capital Book is in its third Edition, as well it deserves to be. I *see* no one with whom to talk about it, except one brave Woman who comes over here at rare intervals—she had read my Atlantic Copy, but must get Bentley's directly it appeared, and she (a woman of remarkably strong and independent Judgment) loves it all—not (as some you know) wishing some of it away. No; she says she wants all to complete her notion of the writer. Nor have I *heard* of any one who thinks otherwise: so 'some people' may be wrong. I know you do not care about all this.

I am getting my 'Tales of the Hall' printed, and shall one day ask you, and three or four beside, whether it had better be published. I think you, and those three or four others, will like it; but they may also judge that indifferent readers might not. And that you will all of you have to tell me when the thing is done. I shall not be in the least disappointed if you tell me to keep it among 'ourselves,' so long as 'ourselves' are pleased; for I know well that Publication would not carry it much further abroad; and I am very well content to pay my money for the little work which I have long meditated doing. I shall have done 'my little owl.' Do you know what that means?—No. Well then; my Grandfather had several Parrots of different sorts and Talents: one of them ('Billy,' I think) could only huff up his feathers in what my Grandfather called an owl fashion; so when Company were praising the more gifted Parrots, he would say—'You will hurt poor Billy's feelings—Come! Do your little owl, my dear!'—You are to imagine a handsome, hair-powdered, Gentleman doing this—and his Daughter— my Mother—telling of it.

And so it is I do my little owl.

This little folly takes a long bit of my Letter paper—and I do not know that you will see any fun in it. Like my Book, it would not tell in Public.

Spedding reads my proofs—for, though I have confidence in my Selection of the Verse (owl), I have but little in my interpolated Prose, which I make obscure in trying to make short. Spedding occasionally marks a blunder; but (confound him!) generally leaves me to correct it.

Come—here is more than enough of my little owl. At night we read Sir Walter for an Hour (Montrose just now) by way of 'Play'—then 'ten minutes' refreshment allowed'—and the Curtain rises on Dickens (Copperfield now) which sends me gaily to bed—after one Pipe of solitary Meditation—in which the—'little owl,' etc.

By the way, in talking of Plays—after sitting with my poor friend and his brave little Wife till it was time for him to turn bedward—I looked in at the famous Lyceum Hamlet; and soon had looked, and heard enough. It was incomparably the worst I had ever witnessed, from Covent Garden down to a Country Barn. I should scarce say this to you if I thought you had seen it; for you told me you thought Irving might have been even a great Actor, from what you saw of his Louis XI. I think. When he got to 'Something too much of this,' I called out from the Pit door where I stood, 'A good deal too much,' and not long after returned to my solitary inn. Here is a very long—and, I believe (as owls go) a rather pleasant Letter. You know you are not bound to repay it in length, even if you answer it at all; which I again vainly ask you not to do if a bore.

I hear from Mrs. Mowbray that our dear Donne is but 'pretty well'; and I am still yours

E. F.G.

LV.

WOODBRIDGE: *April* 25, [1879.]

DEAR MRS. KEMBLE,

I think I have let sufficient time elapse before asking you for another Letter. I want to know how you are: and, if you can tell me that you are as well as you and I now expect to be—anyhow, well rid of that Whooping Cough—that will be news enough for one Letter. What else, you shall add of your own free will:—not feeling bound.

When you last wrote me from Leamington, you crossed over your Address: and I (thinking perhaps of America) deciphered it 'Baltimore.' I wonder the P. O. did not return me my Letter: but there was no Treason in it, I dare say.

My Brother keeps waiting—and hoping—for—Death: which will not come: perhaps Providence would have let it come sooner, were he not rich enough to keep a Doctor in the house, to keep him in Misery. I don't know if I told you in my last that he was ill; seized on by a Disease not uncommon to old Men—an 'internal Disorder' it is polite to say; but I shall say to you, disease of the Bladder. I had always supposed he would be found dead one good morning, as my Mother was—as I hoped to be— quietly dead of the Heart which he had felt for several Years. But no; it is seen good that he shall be laid on the Rack—which he may feel the more keenly as he never suffered Pain before, and is not of a strong Nerve. I will say no more of this. The funeral Bell, which has been at work, as I never remember before, all this winter, is even now, as I write, tolling from St. Mary's Steeple.

'Parlons d'autres choses,' as my dear Sévigné says.

I—We—have finished all Sir Walter's Scotch Novels; and I thought I would try an English one: Kenilworth—a wonderful Drama, which Theatre, Opera, and Ballet (as I once saw it represented) may well reproduce. The Scene at Greenwich, where Elizabeth 'interviews' Sussex and Leicester, seemed to me as fine as what is called (I am told, wrongly) Shakespeare's Henry VIII. [145] Of course, plenty of melodrama in most other parts:—but the Plot wonderful.

Then—after Sir Walter—Dickens' Copperfield, which came to an end last night because I would not let my Reader read the last Chapter. What a touch when Peggotty—the man—at last finds the lost Girl, and—throws a handkerchief over her face when he takes her to his arms—never to leave her! I maintain it—a little Shakespeare—a Cockney Shakespeare, if you will: but as distinct, if not so great, a piece of pure Genius as was born in Stratford. Oh, I am quite sure of that, had I to choose but one of them, I would choose Dickens' hundred delightful Caricatures rather than Thackeray's half-dozen terrible Photographs.

In Michael Kelly's Reminiscences [146] (quite worth reading about Sheridan) I found that, on January 22, 1802, was produced at Drury Lane an Afterpiece called *Urania*, by the Honourable W. Spencer, in which 'the scene of Urania's descent was entirely new to the stage, and produced an extraordinary effect.' Hence then the Picture which my poor Brother sent you to America.

'D'autres choses encore.' You may judge, I suppose, by the N.E. wind in London what it has been hereabout. Scarce a tinge of Green on the hedgerows; scarce a Bird singing (only once the Nightingale, with broken Voice), and no flowers in the Garden but the brave old Daffydowndilly, and Hyacinth—which I scarce knew was so hardy. I am quite pleased to find how comfortably they do in my Garden, and look so Chinese gay. Two of my dear Blackbirds have I found dead—of Cold and Hunger, I suppose; but one is even now singing—across that Funeral Bell. This is so, as I write, and tell you—Well: we have Sunshine at last—for a day— 'thankful for small Blessings,' etc.

I think I have felt a little sadder since March 31 that shut my seventieth Year behind me, while my Brother was—in some such way as I shall be if I live two or three years longer—'Parlons d'autres'—that I am still able to be sincerely yours

E. F.G.

LVI.

MY DEAR MRS. KEMBLE,

By this Post you ought to receive my Crabbe Book, about which I want your Opinion—not as to your own liking, which I doubt not will be more than it deserves: but about whether it is best confined to Friends, who will like it, as you do, more or less out of private prejudice—Two points in particular I want you to tell me;

(1) Whether the Stories generally seem to you to be curtailed so much that they do not leave any such impression as in the Original. That is too long and tiresome; but (as in Richardson) its very length serves to impress it on the mind:—My Abstract is, I doubt not, more readable: but, on that account partly, leaving but a wrack behind. What I have done indeed is little else than one of the old Review Articles, which gave a sketch of the work, and let the author fill in with his better work.

Well then I want to know—(2) if you find the present tense of my Prose Narrative discordant with the past tense of the text. I adopted it partly by way of further discriminating the two: but I may have misjudged: Tell me: as well as any other points that strike you. You can tell me if you will—and I wish you would—whether I had better keep the little *Opus* to ourselves or let it take its chance of getting a few readers in public. You may tell me this very plainly, I am sure; and I shall be quite as well pleased to keep it unpublished. It is only a very, very, little Job, you see: requiring only a little Taste, and Tact: and if they have failed me—*Voilà*! I had some pleasure in doing my little work very dexterously, I thought; and I did wish to draw a few readers to one of my favourite Books which nobody reads. And, now that I look over it, I fancy that I may have missed my aim—only that my Friends will like, etc. Then, I should have to put some Preface to the Public: and explain how many omissions, and some transpositions, have occasioned the change here and there of some initial particle where two originally separated paragraphs are united; some use made of Crabbe's original MS. (quoted in the Son's Edition;) and all such confession to no good, either for my Author or me. I wish you could have just picked up the Book at a Railway Stall, knowing nothing of your old Friend's hand in it. But that cannot be; tell me then, divesting yourself of all personal Regard: and you may depend upon it you will—save me some further bother, if you bid me let publishing alone. I don't even know of a Publisher: and won't have a favour done me by 'ere a one of them,' as Paddies say. This is a terrible Much Ado about next to Nothing. 'Parlons,' etc.

Blanche Donne wrote me you had been calling in Weymouth Street: that you had been into Hampshire, and found Mrs. Sartoris better—Dear Donne seems to have been pleased and mended by his Children coming about him. I say but little of my Brother's Death. [149] We were very good friends, of very different ways of thinking; I had not been within side his lawn gates (three miles off) these dozen years (no fault of his), and I did not enter them at his Funeral—which you will very likely—and properly— think wrong. He had suffered considerably for some weeks: but, as he became weaker, and (I suppose) some narcotic Medicine—O blessed Narcotic!—soothed his pains, he became dozily happy. The Day before he died, he opened his Bed-Clothes, as if it might be his Carriage Door, and said to his Servant 'Come—Come inside—I am going to meet them.'

Voilà une petite Histoire. Et voilà bien assez de mes Egoïsmes. Adieu, Madame; dites-moi tout franchement votre opinion sur ce petit Livre; ah! vous n'en pouvez parler autrement qu'avec toute franchise—et croyez moi, tout aussi franchement aussi,

Votre ami dévoué
E. F.G.

LVII.

WOODBRIDGE: *May* 22, [1879.]

MY DEAR MRS. KEMBLE,

I must thank you for your letter; I was, beforehand, much of your Opinion; and, unless I hear very different advice from the two others whom I have consulted—Spedding, the All-wise—(I mean that), and Aldis Wright, experienced in the Booksellers' world, I shall very gladly abide by your counsel—and my own. You (I do believe) and a few friends who already know Crabbe, will not be the worse for this 'Handybook' of one of his most diffuse, but (to me) most agreeable, Books. That name (Handybook), indeed, I had rather thought of calling the Book, rather than 'Readings'— which suggests readings aloud, whether private or public—neither of which I intended—simply, Readings to oneself. I, who am a poor reader in any way, have found it all but impossible to read Crabbe to anybody. So much for that—except that, the Portrait I had prepared by way of frontispiece turns out to be an utter failure, and that is another satisfactory reason for not publishing. For I particularly wanted this Portrait, copied from a Picture by Pickersgill which was painted in 1817, when these Tales were a-writing, to correct the Phillips Portrait done in the same year, and showing Crabbe with his company Look—not insincere at all—but not at all representing the *writer*. When Tennyson saw Laurence's Copy of this Pickersgill—here, at my house here—he said—'There I recognise the Man.'

If you were not the truly sincere woman you are, I should have thought that you threw in those good words about my other little Works by way of salve for your *dictum* on this Crabbe. But I know it is not so. I cannot think what 'rebuke' I gave you to 'smart under' as you say. [151a]

If you have never read Charles Tennyson (Turner's) Sonnets, I should like to send them to you to read. They are not to be got now: and I have entreated Spedding to republish them with Macmillan, with such a preface of his own—congenial Critic and Poet—as would discover these Violets now modestly hidden under the rank Vegetation of Browning, Swinburne, and Co. Some of these Sonnets have a Shakespeare fancy in them:—some rather puerile—but the greater part of them, pure, delicate, beautiful, and quite original. [151b] I told Mr. Norton (America) to get them published over the water if no one will do so here.

Little did I think that I should ever come to relish—old Sam Rogers! But on taking him up the other day (with Stothard's Designs, to be sure!) I found a sort of Repose from the hatchet-work School, of which I read in the Athenæum.

I like, you know, a good Murder; but in its place—

> 'The charge is prepared; the Lawyers are met—
> The Judges all ranged, a terrible Show' [152]—

only the other night I could not help reverting to that sublime—yes!—of Thurtell, sending for his accomplice Hunt, who had saved himself by denouncing Thurtell—sending for him to pass the night before Execution with perfect Forgiveness—Handshaking—and 'God bless you—God bless you—you couldn't help it—I hope you'll live to be a good man.'

You accept—and answer—my Letters very kindly: but this—pray do think—is an answer—verily by return of Post—to yours.

Here is Summer! The leaves suddenly shaken out like flags. I am preparing for Nieces, and perhaps for my Sister Andalusia—who used to visit my Brother yearly.

Your sincere Ancient
E. F.G.

LVIII.

WOODBRIDGE: *August* 4, [1879].

MY DEAR MRS. KEMBLE:

Two or three days, I think, after receiving your last letter, I posted an answer addrest to the Poste Restante of—Lucerne, was it?—anyhow, the town whose name you gave me, and no more. Now, I will venture through Coutts, unwilling as I am to trouble their Highnesses—with whom my Family have banked for three—if not four—Generations. Otherwise, I do not think they would be troubled with my Accounts, which they attend to as punctually as if I were 'my Lord;' and I am now their last Customer of my family, I believe, though I doubt not they have several Dozens of my Name in their Books—for Better or Worse.

What now spurs me to write is—an Article [153] I have seen in a Number of Macmillan for February, with very honourable mention of your Brother John in an Introductory Lecture on Anglo Saxon, by Professor Skeat. If you have not seen this 'Hurticle' (as Thackeray used to say) I should like to send it to you; and will so do, if you will but let me know where it may find you.

I have not been away from this place save for a Day or two since last you heard from me. In a fortnight I may be going to Lowestoft along with my friends the Cowells.

I take great Pleasure in Hawthorne's Journals—English, French, and Italian—though I cannot read his Novels. They are too thickly detailed for me: and of unpleasant matter too. We of the Old World beat the New, I think, in a more easy manner; though Browning & Co. do not bear me out there. And I am sincerely yours

E. F.G.

LIX.

LOWESTOFT, *Sept*. 18, [1879.]

MY DEAR MRS. KEMBLE,

Your last letter told me that you were to be back in England by the middle of this month. So I write some lines to ask if you *are* back, and where to be found. To be sure, I can learn that much from some Donne: to the Father of whom I must commit this letter for any further Direction. But I will also say a little—very little having to say—beyond asking you how you are, and in what Spirits after the great Loss you have endured. [154]

Of that Loss I heard from Blanche Donne—some while, it appears, before you heard of it yourself. I cannot say that it was surprising, however sad, considering the terrible Illness she had some fifteen years ago. I will say no more of it, nor of her, of whom I could say so much; but nothing that would not be more than superfluous to you.

It did so happen, that, the day before I heard of her Death, I had thought to myself that I would send her my Crabbe, as to my other friends, and wondered that I had not done so before. I should have sent off the Volume for Donne to transmit when—Blanche's Note came.

After writing of this, I do not think I should add much more, had I much else to write about. I will just say that I came to this place five weeks ago to keep company with my friend Edward Cowell, the Professor; we read Don Quixote together in a morning and chatted for two or three hours of an evening; and now he is gone away to Cambridge and [has] left me to my Nephews and Nieces here. By the month's end I shall be home at Woodbridge, whither any Letter you may please to write me may be addressed.

I try what I am told are the best Novels of some years back, but find I cannot read any but Trollope's. So now have recourse to Forster's Life of Dickens—a very good Book, I still think. Also, Eckermann's Goethe— almost as repeatedly to be read as Boswell's Johnson—a German Johnson—and (as with Boswell) more interesting to me in Eckermann's Diary than in all his own famous works.

Adieu: Ever yours sincerely
E. F.G.

I am daily—hourly—expecting to hear of the Death of another Friend [155]—not so old a Friend, but yet a great loss to me.

LX.

11 MARINE TERRACE, LOWESTOFT,
Septr. 24, [1879]

MY DEAR MRS. KEMBLE,

I was to have been at Woodbridge before this: and your Letter only reached me here yesterday. I have thought upon your desire to see me as an old Friend of yourself and yours; and you shall not have the trouble of saying so in vain. I should indeed be perplext at the idea of your coming all this way for such a purpose, to be shut up at an Hotel with no one to look in on you but myself (for you would not care for my Kindred here)—and my own Woodbridge House would require a little time to set in order, as I have for the present lost the services of one of my 'helps' there. What do you say to my going to London to see you instead of your coming down to see me? I should anyhow have to go to London soon; and I could make my going sooner, or as soon as you please. Not but, if you want to get out of London, as well as to see me, I can surely get my house right in a little time, and will gladly do so, should you prefer it. I hope, indeed, that you will not stay in London at this time of year, when so many friends are out of it; and it has been my thought—and hope, I may say—that you have already betaken yourself to some pleasant place, with a pleasant Friend or two, which now keeps me from going at once to look for you in London, after a few Adieus here. Pray let me know your wishes by return of Post: and I will do my best to meet them immediately: being

Ever sincerely yours
E. F.G.

LXI.

WOODBRIDGE: *Sept.* 28, [1879.]

DEAR MRS. KEMBLE:—

I cannot be sure of your Address: but I venture a note—to say that—If you return to London on Wednesday, I shall certainly run up (the same day, if I can) to see you before you again depart on Saturday, as your letter proposes. [157]

But I also write to beg you not to leave your Daughter for ever so short a while, simply because you had so arranged, and told me of your Arrangement.

If this Note of mine reach you somehow to morrow, there will be plenty of time for you to let me know whether you go or not: and, even if there be not time before Wednesday, why, I shall take no harm in so far as I really have a very little to do, and moreover shall see a poor Lady who has just lost her husband, after nearly three years anxious and uncertain watching, and now finds herself (brave and strong little Woman) somewhat floored now the long conflict is over. These are the people I may have told you of whom I have for some years met here and there in Suffolk—chiefly by the Sea; and we somehow suited one another. [158] He was a brave, generous, Boy (of sixty) with a fine Understanding, and great Knowledge and Relish of Books: but he had applied too late in Life to Painting which he could not master, though he made it his Profession. A remarkable mistake, I always thought, in so sensible a man.

Whether I find you next week, or afterward (for I promise to find you any time you appoint) I hope to find you alone—for twenty years' Solitude make me very shy: but always your sincere

E. F.G.

LXII.

LITTLE GRANGE: WOODBRIDGE. *October* 7, [1879]

DEAR MRS. KEMBLE,

When I got home yesterday, and emptied my Pockets, I found the precious Enclosure which I had meant to show, and (if you pleased) to give you. A wretched Sketch (whether by me or another, I know not) of your Brother John in some Cambridge Room, about the year 1832-3, when he and I were staying there, long after Degree time—he, studying Anglo-Saxon, I suppose—reading something, you see, with a glass of Ale on the table—or old Piano-forte was it?—to which he would sing very well his German Songs. Among them,

Do you remember? I afterwards associated it with some stray verses applicable to one I loved.

> 'Heav'n would answer all your wishes,
>   Were it much as Earth is here;
> Flowing Rivers full of Fishes,
>   And good Hunting half the Year.'

Well:—here is the cause of this Letter, so soon after our conversing together, face to face, in Queen Anne's Mansions. A strange little After-piece to twenty years' Separation.

And now, here are the Sweet Peas, and Marigolds, sown in the Spring, still in a faded Blossom, and the Spirit that Tennyson told us of fifty years ago haunting the Flower-beds, [160] and a Robin singing—nobody else.

And I am to lose my capital Reader, he tells me, in a Fortnight, no Book-binding surviving under the pressure of Bad Times in little Woodbridge. 'My dear Fitz, there is no Future for little Country towns,' said Pollock to me when he came here some years ago.

But my Banker here found the Bond which he had considered unnecessary, safe in his Strong Box:—and I am your sincere Ancient

E. F.G.

Burn the poor Caricature if offensive to you. The 'Alexander' profile was become somewhat tarnished then.

LXIII.

MY DEAR MRS. KEMBLE,

I am glad to think that my Regard for you and yours, which I know to be sincere, is of some pleasure to you. Till I met you last in London, I thought you had troops of Friends at call; I had not reflected that by far the greater number of them could not be Old Friends; and those you cling to, I feel, with constancy.

I and my company (viz. Crabbe, etc.) could divert you but little until your mind is at rest about Mrs. Leigh. I shall not even now write more than to say that a Letter from Mowbray, which tells of the kind way you received him and his Brother, says also that his Father is well, and expects Valentia and Spouse in November.

This is all I will write. You will let me know by a line, I think, when that which you wait for has come to pass. A Post Card with a few words on it will suffice.

You cross over your Address (as usual) but I do my best to find you.

Ever yours
E. F.G.

LXIV.

WOODBRIDGE: *Oct*. [? *Nov.*] 4/79.

MY DEAR LADY:—

I need not tell you that I am very glad of the news your note of Sunday tells me: and I take it as a pledge of old Regard that you told it me so soon: even but an hour after that other Kemble was born. [161]

I know not if the short letter which I addressed to 4 Everton Place, Leamington (as I read it in your former Letter), reached you. Whatever the place be called, I expect you are still there; and there will be for some time longer. As there may be some anxiety for some little time, I shall not enlarge as usual on other matters; if I do not hear from you, I shall conclude that all is going on well, and shall write again. Meanwhile, I address this Letter to London, you see, to make sure of you this time: and am ever yours sincerely

E. F.G.

By the by, I think the time is come when, if you like me well enough, you may drop my long Surname, except for the external Address of your letter. It may seem, but is not, affectation to say that it is a name I dislike; [162] for one reason, it has really caused me some confusion and trouble with other more or less Irish bodies, being as common in Ireland as 'Smith,' etc., here—and particularly with 'Edward'—I suppose because of the patriot Lord who bore [it]. I should not, even if I made bold to wish so to do, propose to treat you in the same fashion; inasmuch as I like your Kemble name, which has become as it were classical in England.

LXV.

WOODBRIDGE: *Nov.* 13/79.

MY DEAR LADY,

Now that your anxieties are, as I hope, over, and that you are returned, as I suppose, to London, I send you a budget. First: the famous *Belvidere Hat*; which I think you ought to stick into your Records. [163a] Were I a dozen years younger, I should illustrate all the Book in such a way; but, as my French song says, 'Le Temps est trop court pour de si longs projets.'

Next, you behold a Photo of Carlyle's Niece, which he bid her send me two or three years ago in one of her half-yearly replies to my Enquiries. What a shrewd, tidy, little Scotch Body! Then you have her last letter, telling of her Uncle, and her married Self, and thanking me for a little Wedding gift which I told her was bought from an Ipswich Pawnbroker [163b]—a very good, clever fellow, who reads Carlyle, and comes over here now and then for a talk with me. Mind, when you return me the Photo, that you secure it around with your Letter paper, that the Postman may not stamp into it. Perhaps this trouble is scarce worth giving you.

'Clerke Sanders' has been familiar to me these fifty years almost; since Tennyson used to repeat it, and 'Helen of Kirkconnel,' at some Cambridge gathering. At that time he looked something like the Hyperion shorn of his Beams in Keats' Poem: with a Pipe in his mouth. Afterwards he got a touch, I used to say, of Haydon's Lazarus. Talking of Keats, do not forget to read Lord Houghton's Life and Letters of him: in which you will find what you may not have guessed from his Poetry (though almost unfathomably deep in that also) the strong, masculine, Sense and Humour, etc., of the man more akin to Shakespeare, I am tempted to think, in a perfect circle of Poetic Faculties, than any Poet since.

Well: the Leaves which hung on more bravely than ever I remember are at last whirling away in a Cromwell Hurricane—(not quite that, neither)—and my old Man says he thinks Winter has set in at last. We cannot complain hitherto. Many summer flowers held out in my Garden till a week ago, when we dug up the Beds in order for next year. So now little but the orange Marigold, which I love for its colour (Irish and Spanish) and Courage, in living all Winter through. Within doors, I am again at my everlasting Crabbe! doctoring his Posthumous Tales *à la mode* of those of 'The Hall,' to finish a Volume of simple 'Selections' from his other works: all which I will leave to be used, or not, whenever old Crabbe rises up again: which will not be in the Lifetime of yours ever

E. F.G.

I dared not decypher all that Mrs. Wister wrote in my behalf—because I knew it must be sincere! Would she care for my Eternal Crabbe?

LXVI.

[*Nov.* 1879.]

MY DEAR LADY,

I must say a word upon a word in your last which really pains me—about yours and Mrs. Wister's sincerity, etc. Why, I do most thoroughly believe in both; all I meant was that, partly from your own old personal regard for me, and hers, perhaps inherited from you, you may both very sincerely over-rate my little dealings with other great men's thoughts. For you know full well that the best Head may be warped by as good a Heart beating under it; and one loves the Head and Heart all the more for it. Now all this is all so known to you that I am vexed you will not at once apply it to what I may have said. I do think that I have had to say something of the same sort before now; and I do declare I will not say it again, for it is simply odious, all this talking of oneself.

Yet one thing more. I did go to London on this last occasion purposely to see you at that particular time: for I had not expected Mrs. Edwards to be in London till a Fortnight afterward, until two or three days after I had arranged to go and meet you the very day you arrived, inasmuch as you had told me you were to be but a few days in Town.

There—there! Only believe me; my sincerity, Madam; and—*Voilà ce qui est fait. Parlons*, etc.

Well: Mrs. Edwards has opened an Exhibition of her husband's works in Bond Street—contrary to my advice—and, it appears, rightly contrary: for over £300 of them were sold on the first private View day, [166] and Tom Taylor, the great Art Critic (who neither by Nature nor Education can be such, 'cleverest man in London,' as Tennyson once said he was), has promised a laudatory notice in the omnipotent Times, and then People will flock in like Sheep. And I am very glad to be proved a Fool in the matter, though I hold my own opinion still of the merit of the Picture part of the Show. Enough! as we Tragic Writers say: it is such a morning as I would not have sacrificed indoors or in letter-writing to any one but yourself, and on the subject named.

BELIEVE ME YOURS SINCERELY.

LXVII.

WOODBRIDGE: *Dec^r*. 10, [1879.]

MY DEAR LADY,

Pray let me know how you have fared thus far through Winter—which began so early, and promises to continue so long. Even in Jersey Fred. Tennyson writes me it is all Snow and N.E. wind: and he says the North of Italy is blocked up with Snow. You may imagine that we are no better off in the East of England. How is it in London, and with yourself in Queen Anne's Mansions? I fancy that you walk up and down that ante-room of yours for a regular time, as I force myself to do on a Landing-place in this house when I cannot get out upon what I call my Quarter-deck: a walk along a hedge by the upper part of a field which 'dominates' (as the phrase now goes) over my House and Garden. But I have for the last Fortnight had Lumbago, which makes it much easier to sit down than to get up again. However, the time goes, and I am surprised to find Sunday come round again. (Here is my funny little Reader come—to give me 'All the Year Round' and Sam Slick.)

Friday.

I suppose I should have finished this Letter in the way it begins, but by this noon's post comes a note from my Brother-in-law, De Soyres, telling me that his wife Andalusia died yesterday. [168] She had somewhile suffered with a weak Heart, and this sudden and extreme cold paralysed what vitality it had. But yesterday I had posted her a Letter re-enclosing two Photographs of her Grand Children whom she was very fond and proud of; and that Letter is too late, you see. Now, none but Jane Wilkinson and E. F.G. remain of the many more that you remember, and always looked on with kindly regard. This news cuts my Letter shorter than it would have been; nevertheless pray let me know how you yourself are: and believe me yours

Ever and truly,
E. F.G.

I have had no thought of going to London yet: but I shall never go in future without paying a Visit to you, if you like it. I know not how Mrs. Edwards' Exhibition of her Husband's Pictures succeeds: I begged her to leave such a scheme alone; I cannot admire his Pictures now he is gone more than I did when he was here; but I hope that others will prove me to be a bad adviser.

LXVIII.

WOODBRIDGE: *Jan.* 8/80.

MY DEAR MRS. KEMBLE,

I think sufficient time has elapsed since my last letter to justify my writing you another, which, you know, means calling on you to reply. When last you wrote, you were all in Flannel; pray let me hear you now are. Certainly, we are better off in weather than a month ago: but I fancy these Fogs must have been dismal enough in London. A Letter which I have this morning from a Niece in Florence tells me they have had 'London Fog' (she says) for a Fortnight there. She says, that my sister Jane (your old Friend) is fairly well in health, but very low in Spirits after that other Sister's Death. I will [not] say of myself that I have weathered away what Rheumatism and Lumbago I had; nearly so, however; and tramp about my Garden and Hedgerow as usual. And so I clear off Family scores on my side. Pray let me know, when you tell of yourself, how Mrs. Leigh and those on the other side of the Atlantic fare.

Poor Mrs. Edwards, I doubt, is disappointed with her Husband's Gallery: not because of its only just repaying its expenses, except in so far as that implies that but few have been to see it. She says she feels as if she had nothing to live for, now that 'her poor Old Dear' is gone. One fine day she went down to Woking where he lies, and—she did not wish to come back. It was all solitary, and the grass beginning to spring, and a Blackbird or two singing. She ought, I think, to have left London, as her Doctor told her, for a total change of Scene; but she may know best, being a very clever, as well as devoted little Woman.

Well—you saw 'The Falcon'? [169] Athenæum and Academy reported of it much as I expected. One of them said the Story had been dramatised before: I wonder why. What reads lightly and gracefully in Boccaccio's Prose, would surely not do well when drawn out into dramatic Detail: two People reconciled to Love over a roasted Hawk; about as unsavoury a Bird to eat as an Owl, I believe. No doubt there was a Chicken substitute at St. James', but one had to believe it to be Hawk; and, anyhow, I have always heard that it is very difficult to eat, and talk, on the Stage—though people seem to manage it easily enough in real Life.

By way of a Christmas Card I sent Carlyle's Niece a Postage one, directed to myself, on the back of which she might [write] a few words as to how he and herself had weathered the late Cold. She replied that he was well: had not relinquished his daily Drives: and was (when she wrote) reading Shakespeare and Boswell's Hebrides. The mention of him reminds me of your saying—or writing—that you felt shy of 'intruding' yourself upon him by a Visit. My dear Mrs. Kemble, this is certainly a mistake (wilful?) of yours; he may have too many ordinary Visitors; but I am quite sure that he would be gratified at your taking the trouble to go and see him. Pray try, weather and flannel permitting.

I find some good Stuff in Bagehot's Essays, in spite of his name, which is simply 'Bagot,' as men call it. Also, I find Hayward's Select Essays so agreeable that I suppose they are very superficial.

At night comes my quaint little Reader with Chambers' Journal, and All [the] Year Round—the latter with one of Trollope's Stories [171]—always delightful to me, and (I am told) very superficial indeed, as compared to George Eliot, whom I cannot relish at all.

Thus much has come easily to my pen this day, and run on, you see, to the end of a second Sheet. So I will 'shut up,' as young Ladies now say; but am always and sincerely yours

E. F.G.

LXIX.

WOODBRIDGE: *Febr.* 3/80.

MY DEAR LADY,

I do not think it is a full month since I last taxed you for some account of yourself: but we have had hard weather, you know, ever since: your days have been very dark in London, I am told, and as we have all been wheezing under them, down here, I want to know how you stand it all. I only hope my MS. is not very bad; for I am writing by Candle, before my Reader comes. He eat such a Quantity of Cheese and Cake between the Acts that he could scarce even see to read at all after; so I had to remind him that, though he was not quite sixteen, he had much exceeded the years of a Pig. Since which we get on better. I did not at all like to have my Dombey spoiled; especially Captain Cuttle, God bless him, and his Creator, now lying in Westminster Abbey. The intended Pathos is, as usual, missed: but just turn to little Dombey's Funeral, where the Acrobat in the Street

- 86 -

suspends his performance till the Funeral has passed, and his Wife wonders if the little Acrobat in her Arms will so far outlive the little Boy in the Hearse as to wear a Ribbon through his hair, following his Father's Calling. It is in such Side-touches, you know, that Dickens is inspired to Create like a little God Almighty. I have read half his lately published letters, which, I think, add little to Forster's Account, unless in the way of showing what a good Fellow Dickens was. Surely it does not seem that his Family were not fond of him, as you supposed?

I have been to Lowestoft for a week to see my capital Nephew, Edmund Kerrich, before he goes to join his Regiment in Ireland. I wish you could see him make his little (six years old) put him through his Drill. That is worthy of Dickens: and I am always yours sincerely—and I do hope not just now very illegibly—

LITTLEGRANGE.

LXX.

WOODBRIDGE: *Febr.* 12/80.

MY DEAR MRS. KEMBLE:

A week ago I had a somewhat poor account of Donne from Edith D.— that he had less than his usually little Appetite, and could not sleep without Chloral. This Account I at first thought of sending to you: but then I thought you would soon be back in London to hear [of] him yourself; so I sent it to his great friend Merivale, who, I thought, must have less means of hearing about him at Ely. I enclose you this Dean's letter: which you will find worth the trouble of decyphering, as all this Dean's are. And you will see there is a word for you which you will have to interpret for me. What is the promised work he is looking for so eagerly? [173] Your Records he 'devoured' a Year ago, as a letter of his then told me; and I suppose that his other word about the number of your Father's house refers to something in those Records. I am not surprised at such an Historian reading your Records: but I was surprised to find him reading Charles Mathews' Memoir, as you will see he has been doing. I told him I had been reading it: but then that is all in my line. Have you? No, I think: nor I, by the way, quite half, and that in Vol. ii.—where is really a remarkable account of his getting into Managerial Debt, and its very grave consequences.

I hear that Mr. Lowell is coming Ambassador to England, after a very terrible trial in nursing (as he did) his Wife: who is only very slowly recovering Mind as well as Body. I believe I wrote all this to you before, as also that I am ever yours

E. F.G.

I cannot remember Pangloss in Candide: only a Pedant Optimist, I think, which became the *soubriquet* of Maupertuis' *Akakia* Optimism; but I have not the book, and do not want to have it.

LXXI.

WOODBRIDGE, *March* 1, [1880.]

MY DEAR LADY,

I am something like my good old friend Bernard Barton, who would begin—and end—a letter to some one who had just gone away from his house. I should not mind that, only you will persist in answering what calls for no answer. But the enclosed came here To-day, and as I might mislay it if I waited for my average time of writing to you, I enclose it to you now. It shows, at any rate, that I do not neglect your Queries; nor does he to whom I refer what I cannot answer myself. [174]

This Wright edits certain Shakespeare Plays for Macmillan: very well, I fancy, so far as Notes go; simply explaining what needs explanation for young Readers, and eschewing all *æsthetic* (now, don't say you don't know what 'æsthetic' means, etc.) æsthetic (detestable word) observation. With this the Swinburnes, Furnivalls, Athenæums, etc., find fault: and a pretty hand they make of it when they try that tack. It is safest surely to give people all the *Data* you can for forming a Judgment, and then leave them to form it by themselves.

You see that I enclose you the fine lines [175] which I believe I repeated to you, and which I wish you to paste on the last page of my Crabbe, so as to be a pendant to Richard's last look at the Children and their play. I know not how I came to leave it out when first printing: for certainly the two passages had for many years run together in my Memory.

Adieu, Madame: non pas pour toujours, j'espère; pas même pour long temps. Cependant, ne vous gênez pas, je vous prie, en répondant à une lettre qui ne vaut—qui ne réclame pas même—aucune réponse: tandis que vous me croyez votre très dévoué

EDOUARD DE PETITGRANGE.

LXXII.

WOODBRIDGE: *March* 26, [1880.]

MY DEAR LADY:

The Moon has reminded me that it is a month since I last went up to London. I said to the Cabman who took me to Queen Anne's, 'I think it must be close on Full Moon,' and he said, 'I shouldn't wonder,' not troubling himself to look back to the Abbey over which she was riding. Well; I am sure I have little enough to tell you; but I shall be glad to hear from you that you are well and comfortable, if nothing else. And you see that I am putting my steel pen into its very best paces all for you. By far the chief incident in my life for the last month has been the reading of dear old Spedding's Paper on the Merchant of Venice: [176] there, at any rate, is one Question settled, and in such a beautiful way as only he commands. I could not help writing a few lines to tell him what I thought; but even very sincere praise is not the way to conciliate him. About Christmas I wrote him, relying on it that I should be most likely to secure an answer if I expressed dissent from some other work of his; and my expectation was justified by one of the fullest answers he had written to me for many a day and year.

I read in one of my Papers that Tennyson had another Play accepted at the Lyceum. I think he is obstinate in such a purpose, but, as he is a Man of Genius, he may surprise us still by a vindication of what seem to me several Latter-day failures. I suppose it is as hard for him to relinquish his Vocation as other men find it to be in other callings to which they have been devoted; but I think he had better not encumber the produce of his best days by publishing so much of inferior quality.

Under the cold Winds and Frosts which have lately visited us—and their visit promises to be a long one—my garden Flowers can scarce get out of the bud, even Daffodils have hitherto failed to 'take the winds,' etc. Crocuses early nipt and shattered (in which my Pigeons help the winds) and Hyacinths all ready, if but they might!

My Sister Lusia's Widower has sent me a Drawing by Sir T. Lawrence of my Mother: bearing a surprising resemblance to—The Duke of Wellington. This was done in her earlier days—I suppose, not long after I was born—for her, and his (Lawrence's) friend Mrs. Wolff: and though, I think, too Wellingtonian, the only true likeness of her. Engravings were made of it—so good as to be facsimiles, I think—to be given away to Friends. I should think your mother had one. If you do not know it, I will bring the Drawing up with me to London when next I go there: or will send it up for your inspection, if you like. But I do not suppose you will care for me to do that.

Here is a much longer letter than I thought for; I hope not troublesome to your Eyes—from yours always and sincerely

LITTLEGRANGE.

I have been reading Comus and Lycidas with wonder, and a sort of awe. Tennyson once said that Lycidas was a touchstone of poetic Taste.

LXXIII.

WOODBRIDGE: *March* 28, [1880.]

MY DEAR MRS. KEMBLE,

No—the Flowers were not from me—I have nothing full-blown to show except a few Polyanthuses, and a few Pansies. These Pansies never throve with me till last year: after a Cartload or two of Clay laid on my dry soil, I suppose, the year before. Insomuch that one dear little Soul has positively held on blowing, more or less confidently, all winter through; when even the Marigold failed.

Now, I meant to have intimated about those Flowers in a few French words on a Postcard—purposely to prevent your answering—unless your rigorous Justice could only be satisfied by a Post Card in return. But I was not sure how you might like my Card; so here is a Letter instead; which I really do beg you, as a favour, not to feel bound to answer. A time will come for such a word.

By the by, you can make me one very acceptable return, I hope with no further trouble than addressing it to me. That 'Nineteenth Century' for February, with a Paper on 'King John' (your Uncle) in it. [179] Our Country Bookseller has been for three weeks getting it for me—and now says he cannot get it—'out of print.' I rather doubt that the Copy I saw on your Table was only lent to you; if so, take no more trouble about it; some one will find me a Copy.

I shall revolve in my own noble mind what you say about Jessica and her Jewels: as yet, I am divided between you, and that old Serpent, Spedding. Perhaps 'That is only his Fancy,' as he says of Shylock. What a light, graceful, way of saying well-considered Truth!

I doubt you are serious in reminding me of my Tumbler on the Floor; and, I doubt not, quite right in being so. This comes of one's living so long either with no Company, or with only free and easy. But I am always the same toward you, whether my Tumbler in the right place or not,

THE LAIRD OF LITTLEGRANGE.

LXXIV.

WOODBRIDGE, *April* 6, [1880.] [180a]

My dear Lady,

I hope my letter, and the Magazine which accompanies it, will not reach you at a time when you have family troubles to think about. You can, however, put letter and Magazine aside at once, without reading either; and, anyhow, I wish once more—in vain, I suppose—that you would not feel bound to acknowledge them.

I think this Atlantic, [180b] which I took in so long as you were embarked on it, was sent me by Mr. Norton, to whom I had sent my Crabbe; and he had, I suppose, shown it to Mr. Woodberry, the Critic. And the Critic has done his work well, on the whole, I think: though not quite up to my mark of praise, nor enough to create any revival of Interest in the Poems. You will see that I have made two or three notes by the way: but you are still less bound to read them than the text.

If you be not bothered, I shall ask you to return me the Magazine. I have some thought of taking it in again, as I like to see what goes on in the literary way in America, and I found their critics often more impartial in their estimation of English Authors than our own Papers are, as one might guess would be the case.

I was, and am, reading your Records again, before this Atlantic came to remind me of you. I have Bentley's second Edition. I feel the Dullness of that Dinner Party in Portland Place [181a] (I know it was) when Mrs. Frere sang. She was somewhile past her prime then (1831), but could sing the Classical Song, or Ballad, till much later in Life. Pasta too, whom you then saw and heard! I still love the pillars of the old Haymarket Opera House, where I used to see placarded MEDEA IN CORINTO. [181b]

And I am still yours sincerely
LITTLEGRANGE.

You are better off in London this black weather.

P.S. Since my letter was written, I receive the promised one from Mowbray: his Father well: indeed, in better health and Spirits than usual: and going with Blanche to Southwell on Wednesday (to-morrow) fortnight.

His London house almost, if not quite, out of Quarantine. But—do not go! say I.

LXXV.

WOODBRIDGE: *April* 23, [1880.]

MY DEAR MRS. KEMBLE,

I was really sorry to hear from you that you were about to move again. I suppose the move has been made by this time: as I do not know whither, I must trouble Coutts, I suppose, to forward my Letter to you; and then you will surely tell me your new Address, and also how you find yourself in it.

I have nothing to report of myself, except that I was for ten days at Lowestoft in company (though not in the house) with Edward Cowell the Professor: with whom, as in last Autumn, I read, and all but finished, the second part of Don Quixote. There came Aldis Wright to join us; and he quite agrees with what you say concerning the Jewel-robbery in the Merchant of Venice. He read me the Play; and very well; thoroughly understanding the text: with clear articulation, and the moderate emphasis proper to room-reading; with the advantage also of never having known the Theatre in his youth, so that he has not picked up the twang of any Actor of the Day. Then he read me King John, which he has some thoughts of editing next after Richard III. And I was reminded of you at Ipswich twenty-eight years ago; and of your Father—his look up at Angiers' Walls as he went out in Act ii. I wonder that Mrs. Siddons should have told Johnson that she preferred Constance to any of Shakespeare's Characters: perhaps I misremember; she may have said Queen Catharine. [183a] I must not forget to thank you for the Nineteenth Century from Hatchard's; Tieck's Article very interesting to me, and I should suppose just in its criticism as to what John Kemble then was. I have a little print of him about the time: in Œdipus—(whose Play, I wonder, on such a dangerous subject?) from a Drawing by that very clever Artist De Wilde: who never missed Likeness, Character, and Life, even when reduced to 16mo Engraving. [183b]

What you say of Tennyson's Eyes reminded me that he complained of the Dots in Persian type flickering before them: insomuch that he gave up studying it. This was some thirty years ago. Talking on the subject one day to his Brother Frederick, he—(Frederick)—said he thought possible that a sense of the Sublime was connected with Blindness: as in Homer, Milton, and Handel: and somewhat with old Wordsworth perhaps; though his Eyes were, I think, rather weak than consuming with any inward Fire.

I heard from Mr. Norton that Lowell had returned to Madrid in order to bring his Wife to London—if possible. She seems very far from being recovered; and (Norton thinks) would not have recovered in Spain: so Lowell will have one consolation for leaving the land of Cervantes and Calderon to come among the English, whom I believe he likes little better than Hawthorne liked them.

I believe that yesterday was the first of my hearing the Nightingale; certainly of hearing *my* Nightingale in the trees which I planted, 'hauts comme ça,' as

Madame de Sévigné says. I am positively about to read her again, 'tout Madame de Sévigné,' as Ste. Beuve said. [184a] What better now Spring is come? [184b] She would be enjoying her Rochers just now. And I think this is a dull letter of mine; but I am always sincerely yours

E. DE PETITGRANGE.

LXXVI.

WOODBRIDGE: *May* 25/80.

MY DEAR LADY,

Another full Moon reminds [me] of my monthly call upon you by Letter— a call to be regularly returned, I know, according to your Etiquette. As so it must be, I shall be very glad to hear that you are better than when you last wrote, and that some, if not all, of the 'trouble' you spoke of has passed away. I have not heard of Donne since that last letter of yours: but a Post Card from Mowbray, who was out holyday-making in Norfolk, tells me that he will write as soon as he has returned to London, which, I think, must be about this very time.

I shall be sorry if you do not get your annual dose of Mountain Air; why can you not? postponing your visit to Hampshire till Autumn—a season when I think those who want company and comfort are most glad of it. But you are determined, I think, to do as you are asked: yes, even the more so if you do not wish it. And, moreover, you know much more of what is fittest to do than I.

A list of Trench's works in the Academy made me think of sending him my Crabbe; which I did: and had a very kind answer from him, together with a Copy of a second Edition of his Calderon Essay and Translation. He had not read any Crabbe since he was a Lad: what he may think of him now I know not: for I bid him simply acknowledge the receipt of my Volume, as I did of his. I think much the best way, unless advice is wanted on either side before publication.

If you write—which you will, unless—nay, whether troubled or not, I think—I should like to hear if you have heard anything of Mr. Lowell in London. I do not write to him for fear of bothering him: but I wish to know that his Wife is recovered. I have been thinking for some days of writing a Note to Carlyle's Niece, enclosing her a Post Card to be returned to me with just a word about him and herself. A Card only: for I do not know how occupied she may be with her own family cares by this time.

I have re-read your Records, in which I do not know that I find any too much, as I had thought there was of some early Letters. Which I believe I told you while the Book was in progress. [186] It is, I sincerely say, a capital Book, and, as I have now read it twice over with pleasure, and I will say, with Admiration—if but for its Sincerity (I think you will not mind my saying that much)—I shall probably read it over again, if I live two years more. I am now embarked on my blessed Sévigné, who, with Crabbe, and John Wesley, seem to be my great hobbies; or such as I do not tire of riding, though my friends may weary of hearing me talk about them.

By the by, to-morrow is, I think, Derby Day; which I remember chiefly for its marking the time when Hampton Court Chestnuts were usually in full flower. You may guess that we in the Country here have been gaping for rain to bring on our Crops, and Flowers; very tantalising have been many promising Clouds, which just dropped a few drops by way of Compliment, and then passed on. But last night, when Dombey was being read to me we heard a good splash of rain, and Dombey was shut up that we might hear, and see, and feel it. [187] I never could make out who wrote two lines which I never could forget, wherever I found them:—

> 'Abroad, the rushing Tempest overwhelms
> Nature pitch dark, and rides the thundering elms.'

Very like Glorious John Dryden; but many others of his time wrote such lines, as no one does now—not even Messrs. Swinburne and Browning.

And I am always your old Friend, with the new name of

LITTLEGRANGE.

LXXVII.

WOODBRIDGE: *June* 23, [1880.]

MY DEAR MRS. KEMBLE,

You smile at my 'Lunacies' as you call my writing periods; I take the Moon as a signal not to tax you too often for your inevitable answer. I have now let her pass her Full: and June is drawing short: and you were to be but for June at Leamington: so—I must have your answer, to tell me about your own health (which was not so good when last you wrote) and that of your Family; and when, and where, you go from Leamington. I shall be sorry if you cannot go to Switzerland.

I have been as far as—Norfolk—on a week's visit (the only visit of the sort I now make) to George Crabbe, my Poet's Grandson, and his two Granddaughters. It was a very pleasant visit indeed; the people all so sensible, and friendly, talking of old days; the Country flat indeed, but green, well-wooded, and well-cultivated: the weather well enough. [188a]

I carried there two volumes of my Sévigné: and even talked of going over to Brittany, only to see her Rochers, as once I went to Edinburgh only to see Abbotsford. But (beside that I probably should not have gone further than talking in any case) a French Guide Book informed me that the present Proprietor of the place will not let it be shown to Strangers who pester him for a view of it, on the strength of those 'paperasses,' as he calls her Letters. [188b] So this is rather a comfort to me. Had I gone, I should also have visited my dear old Frederick Tennyson at Jersey. But now I think we shall never see one another again.

Spedding keeps on writing Shakespeare Notes in answer to sundry Theories broached by others: he takes off copies of his MS. by some process he has learned; and, as I always insist on some Copy of all he writes, he has sent me these, which I read by instalments, as Eyesight permits. I believe I am not a fair Judge between him and his adversaries; first, because I have but little, if any, faculty of critical Analysis; and secondly, because I am prejudiced with the notion that old Jem is Shakespeare's Prophet, and must be right. But, whether right or wrong, the way in which he conducts, and pleads, his Case is always Music to me. So it was even with Bacon, with whom I could not be reconciled: I could not like Dr. Fell: much more so with 'the Divine Williams,' who is a Doctor that I do like.

It has turned so dark here in the last two days that I scarce see to write at my desk by a window which has a hood over it, meant to exclude—the Sun! I have increased my Family by two broods of Ducks, who compete for the possession of a Pond about four feet in diameter: and but an hour ago I saw my old Seneschal escorting home a stray lot of Chickens. My two elder Nieces are with me at present, but I do not think will be long here, if a Sister comes to them from Italy.

Pray let me hear how you are. I am pretty well myself:—though not quite up to the mark of my dear Sévigné, who writes from her Rochers when close on sixty—'Pour moi, je suis d'une si parfaite santé, que je ne comprends point ce que Dieu veut faire de moi.' [190]

But yours always and a Day,
LITTLEGRANGE.

LXXVIII.

[WOODBRIDGE, *July* 24, 1880.]

'Il sera le mois de Juillet tant qu'il plaira à Dieu' writes my friend Sévigné— only a week more of it now, however. I should have written to my friend Mrs. Kemble before this—in defiance of the Moon—had I not been waiting for her Address from Mowbray Donne, to whom I wrote more than a fortnight ago. I hope no ill-health in himself, or his Family, keeps him from answering my Letter, if it ever reached him. But I will wait no longer for his reply: for I want to know concerning you and your health: and so I must trouble Coutts to fill up the Address which you will not instruct me in.

Here (Woodbridge) have I been since last I wrote—some Irish Cousins coming down as soon as English Nieces had left. Only that in the week's interval I went to our neighbouring Aldeburgh on the Sea—where I first saw, and felt, the Sea some sixty-five years ago; a dreary place enough in spite of some Cockney improvements: my old Crabbe's Borough, as you may remember. I think one goes back to the old haunts as one grows old: as the Chancellor l'Hôpital said when he returned to his native Bourdeaux, I think: 'Me voici, Messieurs,' returned to die, as the Hare does, in her ancient 'gîte.' [191] I shall soon be going to Lowestoft, where one of my Nieces, who is married to an Italian, and whom I have not seen for many years, is come, with her Boy, to stay with her Sisters.

Whither are you going after you leave Hampshire? You spoke in your last letter of Scarboro': but I still think you will get over to Switzerland. One of my old Friends—and Flames—Mary Lynn (pretty name) who is of our age, and played with me when we both were Children—at that very same Aldeburgh—is gone over to those Mountains which you are so fond of: having the same passion for them as you have. I had asked her to meet me at that Aldeburgh—'Aldbro'—that we might ramble together along that beach where once we played; but she was gone.

If you should come to Lowestoft instead of Scarbro', we, if you please, will ramble together too. But I do not recommend the place—very ugly—on a dirty Dutch Sea—and I do not suppose you would care for any of my People; unless it were my little Niece Annie, who is a delightful Creature.

I see by the Athenæum that Tom Taylor is dead [192a]—the 'cleverest Man in London' Tennyson called him forty years ago. Professor Goodwin, of the Boston Cambridge, is in England, and made a very kind proposal to give me a look on his travels. But I could not let him come out of his way (as it would have been) for any such a purpose. [192b] He wrote that Mrs. Lowell was in better health: residing at Southampton, which you knew well near fifty years ago, as your Book tells. Mr. Lowell does not write to me now; nor is there reason that he should.

Please to make my remembrances to Mr. Sartoris, who scarcely remembers me, but whose London House was very politely opened to me so many years ago. Anyhow, pray let me hear of yourself: and believe me always yours sincerely

LXXIX.

WOODBRIDGE: *Friday*, [30 *July*, 1880.]

MY DEAR LADY,

I send you Mowbray's reply to my letter of nearly three weeks ago. No good news of his Father—still less of our Army (news to me told to-day) altogether a sorry budget to greet you on your return to London. But the public news you knew already, I doubt not: and I thought as well to tell you of our Donne at once.

I suppose one should hardly talk of anything except this Indian Calamity: [193] but I am selfish enough to ignore, as much as I can, such Evils as I cannot help.

I think that Tennyson in calling Tom Taylor the 'cleverest man,' etc., meant pretty much as you do. I believe he said it in reply to something I may have said that was less laudatory. At one time Tennyson almost lived with him and the Wigans whom I did not know. Taylor always seemed to me as 'clever' as any one: was always very civil to me: but one of those toward whom I felt no attraction. He was too clever, I think. As to Art, he knew nothing of it then, nor (as he admits) up to 1852 or thereabout, when he published his very good Memoir of Haydon. I think he was too 'clever' for Art also.

Why will you write of 'If you *bid* me come to Lowestoft in October,' etc., which, you must know, is just what I should not ask you to do: knowing that, after what you say, you would come, if asked, were—(a Bull begins here)—were it ever so unlikely for you. I am going thither next week, to hear much (I dare say) of a Brother in Ireland who may be called to India; and am

Ever yours sincerely,
LITTLEGRANGE.

Why won't you write to me from Switzerland to say where a Letter may find you? If not, the Harvest Moon will pass!

LXXX.

IVY HOUSE, LOWESTOFT:
Septr. 20, [194] [1880.]

MY DEAR MRS. KEMBLE,

Here is a second Full Moon since last I wrote—(Harvest Moon, I think). I knew not where to direct to you before, and, as you remain determined not to apprize me yourself, so I have refused to send through Coutts. You do not lose much.

Here have been for nearly two months Five English Nieces clustered round a Sister who married an Italian, and has not been in England these dozen years. She has brought her Boy of six, who seems to us wonderfully clever as compared to English Children of his Age, but who, she tells us, is counted rather behind his Fellows in Italy. Our meeting has been what is called a 'Success'—which will not be repeated, I think. She will go back to her adopted Country in about a month, I suppose. Do you know of any one likely to be going that way about that time?

Some days ago, when I was sitting on the Pier, rather sad at the Departure [of] a little Niece—an abridgment of all that is pleasant—and good—in Woman—Charles Merivale accosted me—he and his good, unaffected, sensible, wife, and Daughter to match. He was looking well, and we have since had a daily stroll together. We talked of you, for he said (among the first things he did say) that he had been reading your Records again: so I need not tell you his opinion of them. He saw your Uncle in Cato when he was about four years old; and believes that he (J. P. K.) had a bit of red waistcoat looking out of his toga, by way of Blood. I tell him he should call on you and clear up that, and talk on many other points.

Mowbray Donne wrote me from Wales a month ago that his Father was going on pretty well. I asked for further from Mowbray when he should have returned from Wales: but he has not yet written. Merivale, who is one of Donne's greatest Friends, has not heard of him more lately than I.

Now, my dear Mrs. Kemble, I want to hear of you from yourself: and I have told you why it is that I have not asked you before. I fancy that you will not be back in England when this Letter reaches Westminster: but I fancy that it will not be long before you find it waiting on your table for you.

And now I am going to look for the Dean, who, I hope, has been at Church this morning: and though I have not done that, I am not the less sincerely yours

E. F.G.

LXXXI.

WOODBRIDGE: *Oct*. 20, 1880.

MY DEAR MRS. KEMBLE,

I was to have gone to London on Monday with my Italian Niece on her way homeward. But she feared saying 'Farewell' and desired me to let her set off alone, to avoid doing so.

Thus I delay my visit to you till November—perhaps toward the middle of it: when I hope to find you, with your blue and crimson Cushions [197] in Queen Anne's Mansions, as a year ago. Mrs. Edwards is always in town: not at all forgetful of her husband; and there will be our Donne also of whom I hear nothing, and so conclude there is nothing to be told, and with him my Visits will be summed up.

Now, lose not a Day in providing yourself with Charles Tennyson Turner's Sonnets, published by Kegan Paul. There is a Book for you to keep on your table, at your elbow. Very many of the Sonnets I do not care for: mostly because of the Subject: but there is pretty sure to be some beautiful line or expression in all; and all pure, tender, noble, and—original. Old Spedding supplies a beautiful Prose Overture to this delightful Volume: never was Critic more one with his Subject—or, Object, is it? Frederick Tennyson, my old friend, ought to have done something to live along with his Brothers: all who *will* live, I believe, of their Generation: and he perhaps would, if he could, have confined himself to limits not quite so narrow as the Sonnet. But he is a Poet, and cannot be harnessed.

I have still a few flowers surviving in my Garden; and I certainly never remember the foliage of trees so little changed in October's third week. A little flight of Snow however: whose first flight used to quicken my old Crabbe's fancy: Sir Eustace Grey written under such circumstances. [198]

And I am always yours
LITTLEGRANGE

(not 'Markethill' as you persist in addressing me.)

LXXXII.

WOODBRIDGE, *Nov*. 17/80.

MY DEAR LADY,

Here is the Moon very near her Full: so I send you a Letter. I have it in my head you are not in London: and may not be when I go up there for a few days next week—for this reason I think so: viz., that you have not acknowledged a Copy of Charles Tennyson's Sonnets, which I desired Kegan Paul to send you, as from me—with my illustrious Initials on the Fly Leaf: and, he or one of his men, wrote that so it should be, or had been done. It may nevertheless not have been: or, if in part done, the illustrious Initials forgotten. But I rather think the Book was sent: and that you would have guessed at the Sender, Initials or not. And as I know you are even over-scrupulous in acknowledging any such things, I gather that the Book came when you had left London—for Leamington, very likely: and that there you are now. The Book, and your Acknowledgment of it, will very well wait: but I wish to hear about yourself—as also about yours—if you should be among them. I talk of 'next week,' because one of my few Visitors, Archdeacon Groome, is coming the week after that, I believe, for a day or two to my house: and, as he has not been here for two years, I do not wish to be out of the way.

A Letter about a fortnight ago from Mowbray Donne told me that his Father was fairly well: and a Post Card from Mowbray two days ago informed [me] that Valentia was to be in London this present week. But I have wanted to be here at home all this time: I would rather see Donne when he is alone: and I would rather go to London when there is more likelihood of seeing you there than now seems to me. Of course you will not in the slightest way hasten your return to London (if now away from it) for my poor little Visits: but pray let me hear from you, and believe me always the same

E. F.G.

LXXXIII.

WOODBRIDGE: *Dec*. 6, [1880.]

MY DEAR LADY,

I was surprised to see a Letter in your MS. which could not be in answer to any of mine. But the Photos account for it. Thank you: I keep that which I like best, and herewith return the other.

Why will you take into your head that I could suppose you wanting in Hospitality, or any other sort of Generosity! That, at least, is not a Kemble failing. Why, I believe you would give me—and a dozen others—£1000 if you fancied one wanted it—even without being asked. The Law of Mede and Persian is that you *will* take up—a perverse notion—now and then. There! It's out.

As to the Tea—'pure and simple'—with Bread and Butter—it is the only meal I do care to join in:—and this is why I did not see Mowbray Donne, who has not his Dinner till an hour and a half after my last meal is done.

I should very gladly have 'crushed a Cup of Tea' with you that last Evening, coming prepared so to do. But you had Friends coming; and so (as Mrs. Edwards was in the same plight) I went to the Pit of my dear old Haymarket Opera: [200] remembering the very corner of the Stage where

Pasta stood when Jason's People came to tell her of his new Marriage; and (with one hand in her Girdle—a movement (Mrs. Frere said) borrowed from Grassini) she interrupted them with her "Cessate—intesi!"—also when Rubini, feathered hat in hand, began that "Ah te, oh Cara"—and Taglioni hovered over the Stage. There was the old Omnibus Box too where D'Orsay flourished in ample white Waistcoat and Wristbands: and Lady Blessington's: and Lady Jersey's on the Pit tier: and my own Mother's, among the lesser Stars, on the third. In place of all which I dimly saw a small Company of less distinction in all respects; and heard an Opera (*Carmen*) on the Wagner model: very beautiful Accompaniments to no Melody: and all very badly sung except by Trebelli, who, excellent. I ran out in the middle to the dear Little Haymarket opposite—where Vestris and Liston once were: and found the Theatre itself spoilt by being cut up into compartments which marred the beautiful Horse-shoe shape, once set off by the flowing pattern of Gold which used to run round the house.

Enough of these Old Man's fancies—But—Right for all that!

I would not send you Spedding's fine Article [201a] till you had returned from your Visit, and also had received Mrs. Leigh at Queen Anne's. You can send it back to me quite at your leisure, without thinking it necessary to write about it.

It is so mild here that the Thrush sings a little, and my Anemones seem preparing to put forth a blossom as well as a leaf. Yesterday I was sitting on a stile by our River side.

You will doubtless see Tennyson's new Volume, [201b] which is to my thinking far preferable to his later things, though far inferior to those of near forty years ago: and so, I think, scarce wanted. There is a bit of Translation from an old War Song which shows what a Poet can do when he condescends to such work: and I have always said that 'tis for the old Poets to do some such service for their Predecessors. I hope this long letter is tolerably legible: and I am in very truth

Sincerely yours
THE LAIRD OF LITTLEGRANGE.

LXXXIV.

WOODBRIDGE, *Christmas Day*, [1880.]

MY DEAR LADY:

You are at Leamington for this day, I expect: but, as I am not sure of your address there, I direct to Queen Anne as usual. This very morning I had a letter from my dear George Crabbe, telling me that he has met your friend

Mr. H. Aïdé at Lord Walsingham's, the Lord of G. C.'s parish: and that Mr. Aïdé had asked him (G. C.) for his copy of my Crabbe. I should have been very glad to give him one had he, or you, mentioned to me that he had any wish for the book: I am only somewhat disappointed that so few do care to ask for it.

I am here all alone for my Christmas: which is not quite my own fault. A Nephew, and a young London clerk, were to have come, but prevented; even my little Reader is gone to London for his Holyday, and left me with Eyes more out of *Kelter* [202] than usual to entertain myself with. 'These are my troubles, Mr. Wesley,' as a rich man complained to him when his Servant put too many Coals on the fire. [203a] On Friday, Aldis Wright comes for two days, on his road to his old home Beccles: and I shall leave him to himself with Books and a Cigar most part of the Day, and make him read Shakespeare of a night. He is now editing Henry V. for what they call the Clarendon Press. He still knows nothing of Mr. Furness, who, he thinks, must be home in America long ago.

Spedding writes me that Carlyle is now so feeble as to be carried up and down stairs. But very 'quiet,' which is considered a bad sign; but, as Spedding says, surely much better than the other alternative, into which one of Carlyle's temperament might so probably have fallen. Nay, were it not better for all of us? Mr. Froude is most constantly with him.

If this Letter is forwarded you, I know that it will not be long before I hear from you. And you know that I wish to hear that all is well with you, and that I am always yours

E. F.G.

How is Mr. Sartoris? And I see a Book of *hers* advertised. [203b]

LXXXV.

WOODBRIDGE: *Jan.* 17, [1881.]

DEAR MRS. KEMBLE,

The Moon has passed her Full: but my Eyes have become so troubled since Christmas that I have not written before. All Christmas I was alone: Aldis Wright came to me on New Year's Day, and read to me, among many other things, 'Winter's Tale' which we could not take much delight in. No Play more undoubtedly, nor altogether, Shakespeare's, but seeming to me written off for some 'occasion' theatrical, and then, I suppose that Mrs. Siddons made much of the Statue Scene.

I cannot write much, and I fancy that you will not care to read much, if you are indeed about to leave Queen Anne. That is a very vexatious business. You will probably be less inclined to write an answer to my letter, than to read it: but answer it you will: and you need trouble yourself to say no more than how you are, and where, and when, you are going, if indeed you leave where you are. And do not cross your letter, pray: and believe me always your sincere old friend

E. F.G.

LXXXVI.

[*Feb.*, 1881.]

MY DEAR LADY:

I expected to send you a piece of Print as well as a Letter this Full Moon. [205] But the Print is not come from the Printer's: and perhaps that is as well: for now you can thank me for it beforehand when you reply (as I know you will) to this Letter—and no more needs to be said. For I do [not] need your Advice as to Publication in this case; no such Design is in my head: on the contrary, not even a Friend will know of it except yourself, Mr. Norton, and Aldis Wright: the latter of whom would not be of the party but that he happened to be here when I was too purblind to correct the few Proofs, and very kindly did so for me. As for Mr. Norton (America), he it was for whom it was printed at all—at his wish, he knowing the MS. had been lying by me unfinisht for years. It is a Version of the two Œdipus Plays of Sophocles united as two Parts of one Drama. I should not send it to you but that I feel sure that, if you are in fair health and spirits, you will be considerably interested in it, and probably give me more credit for my share in it than I deserve. As I make sure of this you see there will be no need to say anything more about it. The Chorus part is not mine, as you will see; but probably quite as good. Quite enough on that score.

I really want to know how you like your new Quarters in dear *old* London: how you are; and whether relieved from Anxiety concerning Mr. Leigh. It was a Gale indeed, such as the oldest hereabout say they do not remember: but it was all from the East: and I do not see why it should have travelled over the Atlantic.

If you are easy on that account, and otherwise pretty well in mind and Body, tell me if you have been to see the Lyceum 'Cup' [206a] and what you make of it. Somebody sent me a Macmillan [206b] with an Article about it by Lady Pollock; the extracts she gave seemed to me a somewhat lame imitation of Shakespeare.

I venture to think—and what is more daring—to write, that my Eyes are better, after six weeks' rest and Blue Glasses. But I say so with due regard to my old Friend Nemesis.

I have heard nothing about my dear Donne since you wrote: and you only said that you had not *heard* a good account of him. Since then you have, I doubt not, seen as well as heard. But, now that I see better (Absit Invidia!) I will ask Mowbray.

It is well, I think, that Carlyle desired to rest (as I am told he did) where he was born—at Ecclefechan, from which I have, or had, several Letters dated by him. His Niece, who had not replied to my note of Enquiry, of two months ago, wrote to me after his Death.

Now I have written enough for you as well as for myself: and am yours always the same

LITTLEGRANGE. *

* 'What foppery is this, sir?'—*Dr. Johnson.*

LXXXVII.

[*Feb.*, 1881.]

MY DEAR MRS. KEMBLE:—

As you generally return a Salute so directly, I began to be alarmed at not hearing from you sooner—either that you were ill, or your Daughter, or some ill news about Mr. Leigh. I had asked one who reads the Newspapers, and was told there had been much anxiety as to the Cunard Ship, which indeed was only just saved from total Wreck. But all is well so far as you and yours are concerned; and I will sing 'Gratias' along with you.

Mowbray Donne wrote to tell me that he and his had provided for some man to accompany our dear old Friend in his walks; and, as he seems himself to like it, all is so far well in that quarter also.

I was touched with the account of Carlyle's simple Obsequies among his own Kinsfolk, in the place of his Birth—it was fine of him to settle that so it should be. I am glad also that Mr. Froude is charged with his Biography: a Gentleman, as well as a Scholar and 'Writer of Books,' who will know what to leave unsaid as well as what to say.

Your account of 'The Cup' is what I should have expected from you: and, if I may say so, from myself had I seen it.

And with this Letter comes my Sophocles, of which I have told you what I expect you will think also, and therefore need not say—unless of a different opinion. It came here I think the same Day on which I wrote to tell you it had not come: but I would not send it until assured that all was well with you. Such corrections as you will find are not meant as Poetical—or rather Versifying—improvements, but either to clear up obscurity, or to provide for some modifications of the two Plays when made, as it were, into one. Especially concerning the Age of Œdipus: whom I do not intend to be the *old* man in Part II. as he appears in the original. For which, and some other things, I will, if Eyes hold, send you some printed reasons in an introductory Letter to Mr. Norton, at whose desire I finished what had been lying in my desk these dozen years.

As I said of my own Æschylus Choruses, I say of old Potter's now: better just to take a hint from them of what they are about—or imagine it for yourself—and then imagine, or remember, some grand Organ piece—as of Bach's Preludes—which will be far better Interlude than Potter—or I—or even (as I dare think) than Sophocles' self!

And so I remain your ancient Heretic,

LITTLE G.

The newly printed Part II. would not bear Ink.

LXXXVIII.

[*Feb.*, 1881.]

MY DEAR LADY,

Pray keep the Book: I always intended that you should do so if you liked it: and, as I believe I said, I was sure that like it you would. I did not anticipate how much: but am all the more glad: and (were I twenty years younger) should be all the more proud; even making, as I do, a little allowance for your old and constant regard to the Englisher. The Drama is, however, very skilfully put together, and very well versified, although that not as an original man—such as Dryden—would have versified it: I will, by and by, send you a little introductory letter to Mr. Norton, explaining to him, a Greek Scholar, why I have departed from so much of the original: 'little' I call the Letter, but yet so long that I did not wish him, or you, to have as much trouble in reading, as I, with my bad Eyes, had in writing it: so, as I tell him—and you—it must go to the Printers along with the Play which it prates about.

I think I once knew why the two Cities in Egypt and Bœotia were alike named Thebes; and perhaps could now find out from some Books now stowed away in a dark Closet which affrights my Eyes to think of. But any of your learned friends in London will tell you, and probably more accurately than Paddy. I cannot doubt but that Sphinx and heaps more of the childish and dirty mythology of Greece came from Egypt, and who knows how far beyond, whether in Time or Space!

Your Uncle, the great John, did enact Œdipus in some Tragedy, by whom I know not: I have a small Engraving of him in the Character, from a Drawing of that very clever artist De Wilde; [210] but this is a heavy Likeness, though it may have been a true one of J. K. in his latter years, or in one of his less inspired—or more asthmatic—moods. This portrait is one of a great many (several of Mrs. Siddons) in a Book I have—and which I will send you if you would care to see it: plenty of them are rubbish such as you would wonder at a sensible man having ever taken the trouble to put together. But I inherit a long-rooted Affection for the Stage: almost as real a World to me as Jaques called it. Of yourself there is but a Newspaper Scrap or two: I think I must have cut out and given you what was better: but I never thought any one worth having except Sir Thomas', which I had from its very first Appearance, and keep in a large Book along with some others of a like size: Kean, Mars, Talma, Duchesnois, etc., which latter I love, though I heard more of them than I saw.

Yesterday probably lighted you up once again in London, as it did us down here. 'Richard' thought he began to feel himself up to his Eyes again: but To-day all Winter again, though I think I see the Sun resolved on breaking through the Snow clouds. My little Aconites—which are sometimes called 'New Year Gifts,' [211a] have almost lived their little Lives: my Snowdrops look only too much in Season; but we will hope that all this Cold only retards a more active Spring.

I should not have sent you the Play till Night had I thought you would sit up that same night to read it. Indeed, I had put it away for the Night Post: but my old Hermes came in to say he was going into Town to market, and so he took it with him to Post.

Farewell for the present—till next Full Moon? I am really glad that all that Atlantic worry has blown over, and all ended well so far as you and yours are concerned. And I am always your ancient

LITTLE G.

LXXXIX. [211b]

[*March*, 1881.]

MY DEAR LADY,

It was very, very good and kind of you to write to me about Spedding. Yes: Aldis Wright had apprised me of the matter just after it happened—he happening to be in London at the time; and but two days after the accident heard that Spedding was quite calm, and even cheerful; only anxious that Wright himself should not be kept waiting for some communication which S. had promised him! Whether to live, or to die, he will be Socrates still.

Directly that I heard from Wright, I wrote to Mowbray Donne to send me just a Post Card—daily if he or his wife could—with but one or two words on it—'Better,' 'Less well,' or whatever it might be. This morning I hear that all is going on even better than could be expected, according to Miss Spedding. But I suppose the Crisis, which you tell me of, is not yet come; and I have always a terror of that French Adage—'*Monsieur se porte mal*— *Monsieur se porte mieux*—*Monsieur est*'—Ah, you know—or you guess, the rest.

My dear old Spedding, though I have not seen him these twenty years and more—and probably should never see him again—but he lives—his old Self—in my heart of hearts; and all I hear of him does but embellish the recollection of him—if it could be embellished—for he is but the same that he was from a Boy—all that is best in Heart and Head—a man that would be incredible had one not known him.

I certainly should have gone up to London—even with Eyes that will scarce face the lamps of Woodbridge—not to see him, but to hear the first intelligence I could about him. But I rely on the Postcard for but a Night's delay. Laurence, Mowbray tells me, had been to see him, and found him as calm as had been reported by Wright. But the Doctors had said that he should be kept as quiet as possible.

I think, from what Mowbray also says, that you may have seen our other old Friend Donne in somewhat worse plight than usual because of his being much shocked at this Accident. He would feel it indeed!—as you do.

I had even thought of writing to tell you of all this, but could not but suppose that you were more likely to know of it than myself; though sometimes one is greatly mistaken with those 'of course you knows, etc.'— But you have known it all: and have very kindly written of it to me, whom you might also have supposed already informed of it: but you took the trouble to write, not relying on 'of course you know, etc.'

I have thought lately that I ought to make some enquiry about Arthur Malkin, who was always very kind to me. I had meant to send him my Crabbe, who was a great favourite of his Father's, 'an excellent companion for Old Age' he told—Donne, I think. But I do not know if I ever did send him the Book, and now, judging by what you tell me, it is too late to do so, unless for Compliment.

The Sun, I see, has put my Fire out—for which I only thank him, and will go to look for him himself in my Garden—only with a Green Shade over my Eyes. I must get to London to see you before you move away to Leamington; when I can bear Sun or Lamp without odious blue Glasses, etc. I dare to think those Eyes are better, though not Sun-proof: and I am ever yours

LITTLE G.

XC. [214]

20 *March*, [1881.]

MY DEAR LADY,

I have let the Full Moon pass because I thought you had written to me so lately, and so kindly, about our lost Spedding, that I would not call on you too soon again. Of him I will say nothing except that his Death has made me recall very many passages in his Life in which I was partly concerned. In particular, staying at his Cumberland Home along with Tennyson in the May of 1835. 'Voilà bien long temps de ça!' His Father and Mother were both alive—he, a wise man, who mounted his Cob after Breakfast, and was at his Farm till Dinner at two—then away again till Tea: after which he sat reading by a shaded lamp: saying very little, but always courteous, and quite content with any company his Son might bring to the house so long as they let him go his way: which indeed he would have gone whether they let him or no. But he had seen enough of Poets not to like them or their Trade: Shelley, for a time living among the Lakes: Coleridge at Southey's (whom perhaps he had a respect for—Southey, I mean), and Wordsworth, whom I do not think he valued. He was rather jealous of 'Jem,' who might have done available service in the world, he thought, giving himself up to such Dreamers; and sitting up with Tennyson conning over the Morte d'Arthur, Lord of Burleigh, and other things which helped to make up the two Volumes of 1842. So I always associate that Arthur Idyll with Basanthwaite Lake, under Skiddaw. Mrs. Spedding was a sensible, motherly Lady, with whom I used to play Chess of a Night. And there was an old Friend of hers, Mrs. Bristow, who always reminded me of Miss La Creevy, if you know of such a Person in Nickleby.

At the end of May we went to lodge for a week at Windermere—where Wordsworth's new volume of Yarrow Revisited reached us. W. was then at his home: but Tennyson would not go to visit him: and of course I did not: nor even saw him.

You have, I suppose, the Carlyle Reminiscences: of which I will say nothing except that, much as we outsiders gain by them, I think that, on the whole, they had better have been kept unpublished—for some while at least. As also thinks Carlyle's Niece, who is surprised that Mr. Froude, whom her Uncle trusted above all men for the gift of Reticence, should have been in so much hurry to publish what was left to his Judgment to publish or no. But Carlyle himself, I think, should have stipulated for Delay, or retrenchment, if publisht at all.

Here is a dull and coldish Day after the fine ones we have had—which kept me out of doors as long as they lasted. Now one turns to the Fireside again. To-morrow is Equinox Day; when, if the Wind should return to North East, North East will it blow till June 21, as we all believe down here. My Eyes are better, I presume to say: but not what they were even before Christmas. Pray let me hear how you are, and believe me ever the same

E. F.G.

Oh! I doubted about sending you what I yet will send, as you already have what it refers to. It really calls for no comment from any one who does not know the Greek; those who do would probably repudiate it.

XCI. [216a]

[*April*, 1881.]

MY DEAR MRS. KEMBLE,

Somewhat before my usual time, you see, but Easter [216b] comes, and I shall be glad to hear if you keep it in London, or elsewhere. Elsewhere there has been no inducement to go until To-day: when the Wind, though yet East, has turned to the Southern side of it: one can walk without any wrapper; and I dare to fancy we have turned the corner of Winter at last. People talk of changed Seasons: only yesterday I was reading in my dear old Sévigné, how she was with the Duke and Duchess of Chaulnes at their Château of Chaulnes in Picardy all but two hundred years ago; that is in 1689: and the green has not as yet ventured to show its 'nez' nor a Nightingale to sing. [217] You see that I have returned to her as for some Spring Music, at any rate. As for the Birds, I have nothing but a Robin, who seems rather pleased when I sit down on a Bench under an Ivied Pollard, where I suppose he has a Nest, poor little Fellow. But we have terrible Superstitions about him here; no less than that he always kills his Parents if he can: my young Reader is quite determined on this head: and there lately has been a Paper in some Magazine to the same effect.

My dear old Spedding sent me back to old Wordsworth too, who sings (his best songs, I think) about the Mountains and Lakes they were both associated with: and with a quiet feeling he sings, that somehow comes home to me more now than ever it did before.

As to Carlyle—I thought on my first reading that he must have been '*égaré*' at the time of writing: a condition which I well remember saying to Spedding long ago that one of his temperament might likely fall into. And now I see that Mrs. Oliphant hints at something of the sort. Hers I think an admirable Paper: [218] better than has yet been written, or (I believe) is likely to be written by any one else. Merivale, who wrote me that he had seen you, had also seen Mrs. Procter, who was vowing vengeance, and threatening to publish letters from Carlyle to Basil Montagu full of 'fulsome flattery'—which I do not believe, and should not, I am sorry to say, unless I saw it in the original. I forget now what T. C. says of him: (I have lent the Book out)—but certainly Barry Cornwall told Thackeray he was 'a humbug'—which I think was no uncommon opinion: I do not mean dishonest: but of pretension to Learning and Wisdom far beyond the reality. I must think Carlyle's judgments mostly, or mainly, true; but that he must have 'lost his head,' if not when he recorded them, yet when he left them in any one's hands to decide on their publication. Especially when not about Public Men, but about their Families. It is slaying the Innocent with the Guilty. But of all this you have doubtless heard in London more than enough. 'Pauvre et triste humanité!' One's heart opens again to him at the last: sitting alone in the middle of her Room—'I want to die'—'I want—a Mother.' 'Ah, Mamma Letizia!' Napoleon is said to have murmured as he lay. By way of pendant to this, recurs to me the Story that when Ducis was wretched his mother would lay his head on her Bosom— 'Ah, mon homme, mon pauvre homme!'

Well—I am expecting Aldis Wright here at Easter: and a young London Clerk (this latter I did invite for his short holiday, poor Fellow!). Wright is to read me 'The Two Noble Kinsmen.'

And now I have written more than enough for yourself and me: whose Eyes may be the worse for it to-morrow. I still go about in Blue Glasses, and flinch from Lamp and Candle. Pray let me know about your own Eyes, and your own Self; and believe me always sincerely yours

LITTLEGRANGE.

I really was relieved that you did not write to thank me for the poor flowers which I sent you. They were so poor that I thought you would feel bound so to do, and, when they were gone, repented. I have now some gay Hyacinths up, which make my pattypan Beds like China Dishes.

XCII. [219]

[April, 1881.]

MY DEAR LADY:

This present Letter calls for no answer—except just that which perhaps you cannot make it. If you have that copy of Plays revised by John the Great which I sent, or brought, you, I wish you would cause your Maid to pack it in brown Paper, and send it by Rail duly directed to me. I have a wish to show it to Aldis Wright, who takes an Interest in your Family, as in your Prophet. If you have already dismissed the Book elsewhere—not much liking, I think, the stuff which J. K. spent so much trouble on, I shall not be surprised, nor at all aggrieved: and there is not much for A. W. to profit by unless in seeing what pains your noble Uncle took with his Calling.

It has been what we call down here 'smurring' rather than raining, all day long: and I think that Flower and Herb already show their gratitude. My Blackbird (I think it is the same I have tried to keep alive during the Winter) seems also to have 'wetted his Whistle,' and what they call the 'Cuckoo's mate,' with a rather harsh scissor note, announces that his Partner may be on the wing to these Latitudes. You will hear of him at Mr. W. Shakespeare's, it may be. There must be Violets, white and blue, somewhere about where he lies, I think. They are generally found in a Churchyard, where also (the Hunters used to say) a Hare: for the same reason of comparative security, I suppose.

I am very glad you agree with me about Mrs. Oliphant. That one paper of hers makes me wish to read her Books.

You must somehow, or somewhile, let me know your Address in Leamington, unless a Letter addressed to Cavendish Square will find you there. Always and truly yours

LITTLE G.

XCIII. [221]

May 8, [1881.]

MY DEAR MRS. KEMBLE:

You will not break your Law, though you have done so once—to tell me of Spedding—But now you will not—nor let me know your Address—so I must direct to you at a venture: to Marshall Thompson's, whither I suppose you will return awhile, even if you be not already there. I think, however, that you are not there yet. If still at Leamington, you look upon a sight which I used to like well; that is, the blue Avon (as in this weather it will be) running through buttercup meadows all the way to Warwick—unless those Meadows are all built over since I was there some forty years ago.

Aldis Wright stayed with me a whole week at Easter: and we did very well. Much Shakespeare—especially concerning that curious Question about the Quarto and Folio Hamlets which people are now trying to solve by Action as well as by Discussion. Then we had The Two Noble Kinsmen—which Tennyson and other Judges were assured has much of W. S. in it. Which parts I forget, or never heard: but it seemed to me that a great deal of the Play might be his, though not of his best: but Wright could find him nowhere.

Miss Crabbe sent me a Letter from Carlyle's Niece, cut out from some Newspaper, about her Uncle's MS. Memoir, and his written words concerning it. Even if Froude's explanation of the matter be correct, he ought to have still taken any hesitation on Carlyle's part as sufficient proof that the MS. were best left unpublisht: or, at any rate, great part of it. If you be in London, you will be wearied enough with hearing about this.

I am got back to my—Sévigné!—who somehow returns to me in Spring: fresh as the Flowers. These latter have done but badly this Spring, cut off or withered by the Cold: and now parched up by this blazing Sun and dry Wind. If you get my letter, pray answer it and tell me how you are: and ever believe me yours

LITTLEGRANGE.

XCIV.

May, [1881.]

MY DEAR LADY,

If I did not write (as doubtless I ought) to acknowledge the Playbook, I really believe that I thought you would have felt bound to answer my acknowledgment! It came all right, thank you: and A. Wright looked it over: and it has been lying ready to be returned to you whenever you should be returned to London. I assure you that I wish you to keep it, unless it be rather unacceptable than otherwise; I never thought you would endure the Plays themselves; only that you might be interested in your brave Uncle's patient and, I think, just, revision of them. This was all I cared for: and wished to show to A. W. as being interested in all that concerns so noble an Interpreter of his Shakespeare as your Uncle was. If you do not care—or wish—to have the Book again, tell me of some one you would wish to have it: had I wished, I should have told you so at once: but I now give away even what I might have wished for to those who are in any way more likely to be more interested in them than myself, or are likely to have a few more years of life to make what they may of them. I do not think that A. W. is one of such: he thought (as you may do) of so much pains wasted on such sorry stuff.

So far from disagreeing with you about Shakespeare emendations, etc., I have always been of the same mind: quite content with what pleased myself, and, as to the elder Dramatists, always thinking they would be better all annihilated after some Selections made from them, as C. Lamb did.

Mowbray Donne wrote to me a fortnight or so since that his Father was 'pretty well,' but weak in the knees. Three days ago came in Archdeacon Groome, who told me that a Friend of Mowbray's had just heard from him that his Father had symptoms of dropsy about the Feet and Ankles. I have not, however, written to ask; and, not having done so, perhaps ought not to sadden you with what may be an inaccurate report. But one knows that, sooner or later, some such end must come; and that, in the meanwhile, Donne's Life is but little preferable to that which promises the speedier end to it.

We are all drying up here with hot Sun and cold Wind; my Water-pot won't keep Polyanthus and Anemone from perishing. I should have thought the nightly Frosts and Winds would have done for Fruit as well as Flower: but I am told it is not so as yet: and I hope for an honest mess of Gooseberry Fool yet. In the meanwhile, 'Ce sera le mois de Mai tant qu'il plaira à Dieu,' and I am always your ancient

LITTLE G.

XCV.

WOODBRIDGE: TUESDAY:
[*End of May*, 1881.]

MY DEAR MRS. KEMBLE:

I must write you a word of 'God Speed' before you go: before even you go to London to prepare for going: for, if I wait till then, you will be all bother with preparations, and leave-takings; and nevertheless feel yourself bound to answer. Pray do not, even if (as I suppose) still at Leamington; for you will still have plenty to think about with Daughter and Children. I do not propose to go to London to shake hands before you go off: for, as I say, you will have enough of that without me—and my blue Spectacles, which I can only discard as yet when looking on the Grass and young Leaves.

I duly sent your Book to Henry Kemble, as you desired: and received a very polite Note from him in acknowledgment.

And now my house is being pulled about my Ears by preparations for my Nieces next week. And, instead of my leaving the coast clear to Broom and Dust-pan, I believe that Charles Keene will be here from Friday to Monday. As he has long talked of coming, I do not like to put him off now he has really proposed to come, and we shall scramble on somehow. And I will get a Carriage and take him a long Drive into the Country where it is greenest. He is a very good fellow, and has lately lost his Mother, to whom he was a very pious Son; a man who can *reverence*, although a Droll in *Punch*.

You will believe that I wish you all well among your Mountains. George Crabbe has been (for Health's sake) in Italy these last two months, and wrote me his last Note from the Lago Maggiore. My Sister Jane Wilkinson talks of coming over to England this Summer: but I think her courage will fail her when the time comes. If ever you should go to, or near, Florence, she would be sincerely glad to see you, and to talk over other Days. She is not at all obtrusively religious: and I think must have settled abroad to escape some of the old Associations in which she took so much part, to but little advantage to herself or others.

You know that I cannot write to you when you are abroad unless you tell me whither I am to direct. And you probably will not do that: but I do not, and shall [not] cease to be yours always and truly

E. F.G.

XCVI.

[*Nov.* 1881.]

MY DEAR LADY:

I was not quite sure, from your letter, whether you had received mine directed to you in the Cavendish Square Hotel:—where your Nephew told me you were to be found. It is no matter otherwise than that I wish you to know that I had not only enquired if you were returned from abroad, but had written whither I was told you were to be found. Of which enough.

I am sorry you are gone again to Westminster, to which I cannot reconcile myself as to our old London. Even Bloomsbury recalls to me the pink May which used to be seen in those old Squares—sixty years ago. But 'enfin, voilà qui est fait.' You know where that comes from. I have not lately been in company with my old dear: Annie Thackeray's Book [227a] is a pretty thing for Ladies in a Rail carriage; but my old Girl is scarce half herself in it. And there are many inaccuracies, I think. Mais enfin, voilà, etc.

Athenæum and Academy advertise your Sequel to Records. [227b] I need not tell you that I look forward to it. I wish you would insert that capital Paper on Dramatic and Theatrical from the Cornhill. [227c] It might indeed very properly, as I thought, have found a place in the Records.

Mowbray Donne wrote me a month ago that his Father was very feeble: one cannot expect but that he will continue to become more and more so. I should run up to London to see him, if I thought my doing so would be any real comfort to him: but *that* only his Family can be to him: and I think he may as little wish to exhibit his Decay to an old Friend, who so long knew him in a far other condition, as his friend might wish to see him so altered. This is what I judge from my own feelings.

I have only just got my Garden laid up for the winter, and planted some trees in lieu of those which that last gale blew down. I hear that Kensington Gardens suffered greatly: how was it with your Green Park, on which you now look down from such a height, and, I suppose, through a London Fog?

Ever yours
LITTLE G.

XCVII.

[*Dec.* 1881.]

MY DEAR MRS. KEMBLE:

I *will* write to you before 1881 is gone, carrying Christmas along with him. A dismal Festivity it always seems to me—I dare say not much merrier to you. I think you will tell me where, and with whom, you pass it. My own company are to be, Aldis Wright, with whom Shakespeare, etc., a London Clerk, may be—that is, if he can get sufficient Holyday—and one or two Guests for the Day.

I forget if I wrote to you since I had a letter from Hallam Tennyson, telling me of a Visit that he and his Father had been making to Warwickshire and Sherwood. The best news was that A. T. was 'walking and working as usual.'

Why, what is become of your Sequel? I see no more advertisement of it in Athenæum and Academy—unless it appears in the last, which I have not conned over. Somehow I think it not impossible—or even unlikely—that you—may—have—withdrawn—for some reason of your own. You see that I speak with hesitation—meaning no offence—and only hoping for my own, and other sakes that I am all astray.

We are reading Nigel, which I had not expected to care for: but so far as I got—four first Chapters—makes me long for Night to hear more. That return of Richie to his Master, and dear George Heriot's visit just after! Oh, Sir Walter is not done for yet by Austens and Eliots. If one of his Merits were not his *clear Daylight*, one thinks, there ought to be Societies to keep his Lamp trimmed as well as—Mr. Browning. He is The Newest Shakespeare Society of Mr. Furnivall.

The Air is so mild, though windy, that I can even sit abroad in the Sunshine. I scarce dare ask about Donne; neither you, nor Mowbray—I dare say I shall hear from the latter before Christmas. What you wrote convinced me there was no use in going up only to see him—or little else—so painful to oneself and so little cheering to him! I do think that he is best among his own.

But I do not forget him—'No!'—as the Spaniards say. Nor you, dear Mrs. Kemble, being your ancient Friend (with a new name) LITTLEGRANGE!

What would you say of the Œdipus, not of Sophocles, but of Dryden and Nat Lee, in which your uncle acted!

P.S. You did not mention anything about your Family, so I conclude that all is well with them, both in England and America.

I wish you would just remember me to Mr. H. Aïdé, who was very courteous to me when I met him in your room.

This extra Paper is, you see, to serve instead of crossing my Letter.

XCVIII. [230]

[*Feb.* 1882.]

MY DEAR MRS. KEMBLE:

This week I was to have been in London—for the purpose of seeing—or offering to see—our dear Donne. For, when they told him of my offer, he said he should indeed like it much—'if he were well enough.' Anyhow, I can but try, only making him previously understand that he is not to make any effort in the case. He is, they tell me, pleased with any such mark of remembrance and regard from his old Friends. And I should have offered to go before now, had I not judged from your last account of him that he was better left with his Family, for his own sake, as well [as] for that of his Friends. However, as I said, I should have gone up on Trial even now, but that I have myself been, and am yet, suffering with some sort of Cold (I think, from some indications, Bronchial) which would ill enable me to be of any use if I got to London. I can't get warm, in spite of Fires, and closed doors, so must wait, at any rate, to see what another week will do for me.

I shall, of course, make my way to Queen Anne's, where I should expect to find you still busy with your Proof-sheets, which I am very glad to hear of as going on. What could have put it into my head even to think otherwise? Well, more unlikely things might have happened—even with Medes and Persians. I do not think you will be offended at my vain surmises.

I see my poor little Aconites—'New Year's Gifts'—still surviving in the Garden-plot before my window; 'still surviving,' I say, because of their having been out for near a month agone. I believe that Messrs. Daffodil, Crocus and Snowdrop are putting in appearance above ground: but (old Coward) I have not put my own old Nose out of doors to look for them.

I read (Eyes permitting) the Correspondence between Goethe and Schiller (translated) from 1798 to 1806 [231]—extremely interesting to me, though I do not understand—and generally skip—the more purely Æsthetic Part: which is the Part of Hamlet, I suppose. But, in other respects, two such men so freely discussing together their own, and each other's, works interest me greatly. At Night, we have The Fortunes of Nigel; a little of it—and not every night: for the reason that I do not wish to eat my Cake too soon. The last night but one I sent my Reader to see Macbeth played by a little 'Shakespearian' company at a Lecture Hall here. He brought me one new Reading—suggested, I doubt not, by himself, from a remembrance of Macbeth's tyrannical ways: 'Hang out our *Gallows* on the outward walls.' Nevertheless, the Boy took great Interest in the Play; and I like to encourage him in Shakespeare, rather than in the Negro Melodists.

Such a long Letter as I have written (and, I doubt, ill written) really calls for Apology from me, busy as you may be with those Proofs. But still believe me sincerely yours

Though Laird of LITTLEGRANGE.

XCIX.

[*Feb.* 1882.]

MY DEAR LADY:—

The same Post which brought me your very kind Letter, brought me also the enclosed.

The writer of it—Mr. Schütz Wilson—a *Littérateur général*—I believe— wrote up Omar Khayyâm some years ago, and, I dare say, somewhat hastened another (and so far as I am concerned) final Edition. Of his Mr.

Terriss I did not know even by name, till Mr. Wilson told me. So now you can judge and act as you see fit in the matter.

If Terriss and Schütz W. fail in knowing your London 'habitat,' you see that the former makes amends in proposing to go so far as Cheltenham to ask advice of you. Our poor dear Donne would have been so glad, and so busy, in telling what he could in the matter—if only in hope of keeping up your Father's Tradition.

I am ashamed to advert to my own little ailments, while you, I doubt not, are enduring worse. I should have gone to London last week had I believed that a week earlier or later mattered; as things are, I will not reckon on going before next week. I want to be well enough to 'cut about' and see the three friends whom I want to see—yourself among the number.

Blakesley (Lincoln's Dean) goes to stay in London next week, and hopes to play Whist in Weymouth Street.

Kegan Paul, etc., publish dear Spedding's 'Evenings,' [233] etc., and never was Book more worth reading—and buying. I think I understand your weariness in bringing out your Book: but many will be the Gainers:— among them yours always

LITTLEG.

C.

[*Feb.* 1882.]

MY DEAR MRS. KEMBLE:

I have quoted, and sent to Mr. Schütz Wilson, just thus much of your Letter, leaving his Friend to judge whether it is sufficiently encouraging to invite him to call on you. I suppose it is: but I thought safest to give your *ipsissima verba.*

'It is so perfectly easy for any one in London to obtain my Address, that I think I may leave the future Mercutio to do so at his leisure or pleasure.'

I dare say you are pretty much indifferent whether he ventures or not; if he does, I can only hope that he is a Gentleman, and if he be so, I do not think you will be sorry to help him in trying to keep up your Father's traditionary excellence in the part, and to save Mr. Terriss—to save Mercutio—from the contagion of Mr. Irving's treatment of Shakespeare— so far as I have seen of it—which is simply two acts of Hamlet.

As I told you, I know nothing—even hitherto heard nothing of Mr. Terriss. His friend, S. Wilson, I have never seen neither. And I hope you will think I have done fairly well in my share of the Business.

Fanny Kerrich, my Niece, and a capital Woman, comes to me to-day, not more for the purpose of seeing myself, than my Brother's Widow who lives alone in a dismal place three miles off. [234a] I am still wheezy, and want to get in order so as to visit my few friends in London next week. [234b]

You see there is no occasion for you to answer this: for, even if I have done amiss, it is past recall; and I am none the less ancient Friend

LITTLEG.!

CI.

[*March*, 1882.]

MY DEAR LADY,

It is very kind of you to break through your rule of Correspondence, that you may tell me how it was with you that last Evening. I was aware of no 'stupidity' on your side: I only saw that you were what you called 'a little tired, and unwell.' Had I known how much, I should of course have left you with a farewell shake of hands at once. And in so far I must blame you. But I blame myself for rattling on, not only then, but always, I fear, in a manner that you tell me (and I thank you for telling me) runs into occasional impertinence—which no length of acquaintance can excuse, especially to a Lady. You will think that here is more than enough of this. But pray do you also say no more about it. I know that you regard me very kindly, as I am sure that I do you, all the while.

And now I have something to say upon something of a like account; about that Mr. Schütz Wilson, who solicited an Introduction to you for his Mercutio, and then proposed to you to avail *himself* of it. That I thought he had better have waited for, rather than himself proposed; and I warned you that I had been told of his being somewhat of a 'prosateur' at his Club. You, however, would not decline his visit, and would encourage him, or not, as you saw fit.

And now the man has heaped coals of fire on my head. Not content with having formerly appraised that Omar in a way that, I dare say, advanced him to another Edition: he (S.W.) now writes me that he feels moved to write in favour of another Persian who now accompanies Omar in his last Avatar! I have told him plainly that he had better not employ time and talent on what I do not think he will ever persuade the Public to care about—but he thinks he will. [236] He may very likely cool upon it: but, in the meanwhile, such are his good Intentions, not only to the little Poem, but, I believe, to myself also—personally unknown as we are to one another. Therefore, my dear Lady, though I cannot retract what I told you on such authority as I had,—nevertheless, as you were so far prejudiced in his favour because of such service as he formerly was to me, I feel bound to tell you of this fresh offer on his part: so that, as you were not unwilling to receive him on trial before, you may not be less favourably disposed toward him now; in case he should call—which I doubt not he will do; though be pleased to understand that I have no more encouraged him to do so now than at first I did.

What a long Story!—I still chirp a little in my throat; but go my ways abroad by Night as well as by Day: even sitting out, as only last night I did. The S.W. wind that is so mild, yet sweeps down my garden in a way that makes havoc of Crocus and Snowdrop; Messrs. Daffodil and Hyacinth stand up better against it.

I hear that Lord Houghton has been partly paralysed; but is up again. Thompson, Master of Trinity, had a very slight attack of it some months ago; I was told Venables had been ill, but I know not of what, nor how much; and all these my contemporaries; and I, at any rate, still yours as ever

E. F.G.

CII.

LITTLEGRANGE: WOODBRIDGE,
March 31, [1882.]

DEAR MRS. KEMBLE:—

It is not yet full Moon: [237a]—but it is my 74th Birthday: and you are the only one whom I write to on that great occasion. A good Lady near here told me she meant to pay me a visit of congratulation: and I begged her to stay at home, and neither say, nor write, anything about it. I do not know that [I] have much to say to you now that I am inspired; but it occurred to me that you might be going away somewhere for Easter, and so I would try to get a word from you concerning yourself before you left London.

The Book? 'Ready immediately' advertised Bentley near a fortnight ago: to-morrow's Academy or Athenæum will perhaps be talking of it to-morrow: of all which you will not read a word, I 'guess.' I think you will get out of London for Easter, if but to get out of the way. Or are you too indifferent even for that?

Satiated as you may have been with notices and records of Carlyle, do, nevertheless, look at Wylie's Book [237b] about him: if only for a Scotch

Schoolboy's account of a Visit to him not long before he died, and also the words of his Bequest of Craigenputtock to some Collegiate Foundation. Wylie (of whom I did not read all, or half) is a Worshipper, but not a blind one. He says that Scotland is to be known as the 'Land of Carlyle' from henceforward. One used to hear of the 'Land of Burns'—then, I think, 'of Scott.'

There is already a flush of Green, not only on the hedges, but on some of the trees; all things forwarder, I think, by six weeks than last year. Here is a Day for entering on seventy-four! But I do think, notwithstanding, that I am not much the better for it. The Cold I had before Christmas, returns, or lurks about me: and I cannot resolve on my usual out-of-door liberty. Enough of that. I suppose that I shall have some Company at Easter; my poor London Clerk, if he can find no more amusing place to go to for his short Holyday; probably Aldis Wright, who always comes into these parts at these Seasons—his 'Nazione' being Beccles. Perhaps also a learned Nephew of mine—John De Soyres—now Professor of some History at Queen's College, London, may look in.

Did my Patron, Mr. Schütz Wilson, ever call on you, up to this time? I dare say, not; for he may suppose you still out of London. And, though I have had a little correspondence with him since, I have not said a word about your return—nor about yourself. I saw in my Athenæum or Academy that Mercutio did as usual. Have you seen the Play?

I conclude (from not hearing otherwise from Mowbray) that his Father is much as when I saw him. I do not know if the Papers have reported anything more of Lord Houghton, and I have not heard of him from my few correspondents.

But pray do you tell me a word about Mrs. Kemble; and beg her to believe me ever the same

E. F.G.

CIII.

[*Spring*, 1882.]

MY DEAR MRS. KEMBLE,

I scarce think, judging by my old Recorder the Moon, that it is a month since I last wrote to you. But not far off, neither. Be that as it may, just now I feel inclined to tell you that I lately heard from Hallam Tennyson by way of acknowledgment of the Programme of a Recital of his Father's verse at Ipswich, by a quondam Tailor there. This, as you may imagine, I did for fun, such as it was. But Hallam replies, without much reference to the Reading: but to tell me how his Father had a fit of Gout in his hand while he was in London: and therefore it was that he had not called on you as he had intended. Think of my dear old Fellow with the Gout! In consequence of which he was forbidden his daily allowance of Port (if I read Hallam's scrawl aright), which, therefore, the Old Boy had stuck to like a fine Fellow with a constancy which few modern Britons can boast of. This reminded me that when I was on my last visit to him, Isle of Wight, 1854, he stuck to his Port (I do not mean too much) and asked me, who might be drinking Sherry, if I did not see that his was 'the best Beast of the two.' So he has remained true to his old Will Waterproof Colours— and so he was prevented from calling on you—his hand, Hallam says, swelled up like 'a great Sponge.' Ah, if he did not live on a somewhat large scale, with perpetual Visitors, I might go once more to see him.

Now, you will, I know, answer me (unless your hand be like his!) and then you will tell me how you are, and how your Party whom you were expecting at Leamington when last you wrote. I take for granted they arrived safe, in spite of the Wind that a little alarmed you at the time of your writing. And now, in another month, you will be starting to meet your American Family in Switzerland, if the Scheme you told me of still hold— with them, I mean. So, by the Moon's law, I shall write to you once again before you leave, and you—will once more answer!

I shall say thus much of myself, that I do not shake off the Cold and Cough that I have had, off and on, these four months: I certainly feel as if some of the internal timbers were shaken; which is not to be wondered at, nor complained of. [241a] Tell me how you fare; and believe me

Your sincere as ancient

LITTLEGRANGE.

I now fancy that it must be Bentley who delays your Book, till Ballantine & Co. have blown over. [241b]

CIV.

Whitmonday, [*May 29th*, 1882.]

MY DEAR MRS. KEMBLE,

Not full moon yet, but Whitsun the 29th of May, [241c] and you told me of your expecting to be in Switzerland. And when once you get there, it is all over with full moons as far as my correspondence with you is concerned.

I heard from Mowbray that his Father had been all but lost to him: but had partially recovered. Not for long, I suppose: nor need I hope: and this is all I will say to you on this subject.

I have now Charles Keene staying Whitsuntide with me, and was to have had Archdeacon Groome to meet him; but he is worn out with Archidiaconal Charges, and so cannot come. But C. K. and I have been out in Carriage to the Sea, and no visitor, nor host, could wish for finer weather.

But this of our dear Donne over-clouds me a little, as I doubt not it does you. Mowbray was to have come down for three days just now to a Friend five miles off: but of course—you know.

Somehow I am at a loss to write to you on such airy topics as usual. Therefore, I shall simply ask you to let me know, in as few lines as you care to write, when you leave England: and to believe me, wherever you go,

Your sincere Ancient
E. F.G.

CV.

WOODBRIDGE, *June* 24, [1882.]

MY DEAR MRS. KEMBLE,

You wrote me that you had bidden Blanche to let you know about her Father: and this I conclude that she, or some of her family have done. Nevertheless, I will make assurance doubly sure by enclosing you the letters I received from Mowbray, according to their dates: and will send them— for once—through Coutts, in hopes that he may find you, as you will not allow me to do without his help. Of that Death [243a] I say nothing: as you may expect of me, and as I should expect of you also; if I may say so.

I have been to pay my annual Visit to George Crabbe and his Sisters in Norfolk. And here is warm weather come to us at last (as not unusual after the Longest Day), and I have almost parted with my Bronchial Cold— though, as in the old Loving Device of the open Scissors, 'To meet again.' I can only wonder it is no worse with me, considering how my contemporaries have been afflicted.

I am now reading Froude's Carlyle, which seems to me well done. Insomuch, that I sent him all the Letters I had kept of Carlyle's, to use or not as he pleased, etc. I do not think they will be needed among the thousand others he has: especially as he tells me that his sole commission is, to edit Mrs. Carlyle's Letters, for which what he has already done is preparatory: and when this is completed, he will add a Volume of personal Recollections of C. himself. Froude's Letter to me is a curious one: a sort of vindication (it seems to me) of himself—quite uncalled for by me, who did not say one word on the subject. [243b] The job, he says, was forced upon him: 'a hard problem'—No doubt—But he might have left the Reminiscences unpublisht, except what related to Mrs. C.—in spite of Carlyle's oral injunction which reversed his written. Enough of all this!

Why will you not 'initiate' a letter when you are settled for a while among your Mountains? Oh, ye Medes and Persians! This may be impertinent of me: but I am ever yours sincerely

E. F.G.

I see your Book advertised as 'ready.'

CVI. [245a]

[*August*, 1882.]

MY DEAR MRS. KEMBLE,

I have let the Full Moon [245b] go by, and very well she looked, too—over the Sea by which I am now staying. Not at Lowestoft: but at the old extinguished Borough of Aldeburgh, to which—as to other 'premiers Amours,' I revert—where more than sixty years ago I first saw, and first felt, the Sea—where I have lodged in half the houses since; and where I have a sort of traditional acquaintance with half the population. 'Clare Cottage' is where I write from; two little rooms—enough for me—a poor civil Woman pleased to have me in them—oh, yes,—and a little spare Bedroom in which I stow a poor Clerk, with his Legs out of the window from his bed—like a Heron's from his nest—but rather more horizontally. We dash about in Boats whether Sail or Oar—to which latter I leave him for his own good Exercise. Poor fellow, he would have liked to tug at that, or rough-ride a horse, from Boyhood: but must be made Clerk in a London Lawyer's Office: and so I am glad to get him down for a Holyday when he can get one, poor Fellow!

The Carlyle 'Reminiscences' had long indisposed me from taking up the Biography. But when I began, and as I went on with that, I found it one of the most interesting of Books: and the result is that I not only admire and respect Carlyle more than ever I did: but even love him, which I never thought of before. For he loved his Family, as well as for so long helped to maintain them out of very slender earnings of his own; and, so far as these two Volumes show me, he loved his Wife also, while he put her to the work which he had been used to see his own Mother and Sisters fulfil, and which was suitable to the way of Life which he had been used to. His indifference to her sufferings seems to me rather because of Blindness than Neglect; and I think his Biographer has been even a little too hard upon him on the score of Selfish disregard of her. Indeed Mr. Norton wrote to me that he looked on Froude as something of an Iago toward his Hero in respect of all he has done for him. The publication of the Reminiscences is indeed a mystery to me: for I should [have] thought that, even in a mercantile point of view, it would indispose others, as me it did, to the Biography. But Iago must have bungled in his work so far as I, for one, am concerned, if the result is such as I find it—or unless I am very obtuse indeed. So I tell Mr. Norton; who is about to edit Carlyle's Letters to Emerson, and whom I should not like to see going to his work with such an 'Animus' toward his Fellow-Editor.

Yours always,
E. F.G.

Faites, s'il vous plait, mes petits Compliments à Madame Wister.

CVII. [247]

ALDEBURGH: *Sept.* 1, [1882.]

MY DEAR MRS. KEMBLE,

Still by the Sea—from which I saw *The Harvest Moon* rise for her three nights' Fullness. And to-day is so wet that I shall try and pay you my plenilunal due—not much to your satisfaction; for the Wet really gets into one's Brain and Spirits, and I have as little to write of as ever any Full Moon ever brought me. And yet, if I accomplish my letter, and 'take it to the Barber's,' where I sadly want to go, and, after being wrought on by him, post my letter—why, you will, by your Laws, be obliged to answer it. Perhaps you may have a little to tell me of yourself in requital for the very little you have to hear of me.

I have made a new Acquaintance here. Professor Fawcett (Postmaster General, I am told) married a Daughter of one Newson Garrett of this Place, who is also Father of your Doctor Anderson. Well, the Professor (who was utterly blinded by the Discharge of his Father's Gun some twenty or twenty-five years ago) came to this Lodging to call on Aldis Wright; and, when Wright was gone, called on me, and also came and smoked a Pipe one night here. A thoroughly unaffected, unpretending, man; so modest indeed that I was ashamed afterwards to think how I had harangued him all the Evening, instead of getting him to instruct me. But I would not ask him about his Parliamentary Shop: and I should not have understood his Political Economy: and I believe he was very glad to be talked to instead, about some of those he knew, and some whom I had known. And, as we were both in Crabbe's Borough, we talked of him: the Professor, who had never read a word, I believe, about him, or of him, was pleased to hear a little; and I advised him to buy the Life written by Crabbe's Son; and I would give him my Abstract of the Tales of the Hall, by way of giving him a taste of the Poet's self.

Yes; you must read Froude's Carlyle above all things, and tell me if you do not feel as I do about it. Professor Norton persists [248] in it that I am proof against Froude's invidious insinuations simply because of my having previously known Carlyle. But how is it that I did not know that Carlyle was so good, grand, and even loveable, till I read the Letters, which Froude now edits? I regret that I did not know what the Book tells us while Carlyle was alive; that I might have loved him as well as admired him. But Carlyle never spoke of himself in that way: I never heard him advert to his Works and his Fame, except one day he happened to mention 'About the time when Men began to talk of me.'

I do not know if I told you in my last that (as you foretold me would be the case) I did not find your later Records so interesting as the earlier. Not from any falling off of the recorder, but of the material.

The two dates of this Letter arise from my having written this second half-sheet so badly that I resolved to write it over again—I scarce know whether for better or worse. I go home this week, expecting Charles Keene at Woodbridge for a week. Please to believe me (with Compliments to Mrs. Wister)

Yours sincerely always
E. F.G.

CVIII. [249]

WOODBRIDGE: *Oct.* 17, [1882.]

MY DEAR MRS. KEMBLE,

I suppose that you are returned from the Loire by this time; but as I am not sure that you have returned to the 'Hotel des Deux Mondes,' whence you dated your last, I make bold once more to trouble Coutts with adding your Address to my Letter. I think I shall have it from yourself not long after. I shall like to hear a word about my old France, dear to me from childish associations; and in particular of the Loire endeared to me by Sévigné—for I never saw the glimmer of its Waters myself. If you were in England I should send you an account of a tour there, written by a Lady in 1833— written in the good old way of Ladies' writing, without any of the smartness, and not too much of the 'graphic' of later times. Did you look at Les Rochers, which, I have read, is not to be looked *into* by the present owner? [250a]

Now for my 'Story, God bless you,' etc., you may guess where none is to be told. Only, my old Housekeeper here has been bedded for this last month, an illness which has caused her great pain, and at one time seemed about to make an End of her. So it may do still: but for the last few days she has suffered less pain, and so we—hope. This has caused much trouble in my little household, as you may imagine—as well on our own account, as on hers.

Mowbray Donne wrote me that his Edith had been seriously—I know not if dangerously—ill; and he himself much out of sorts, having never yet (he says, and I believe) recovered from his Father's death. Blanche, for the present, is quartered at Friends' and Kinsfolk's houses.

Aldis Wright has sent me a Photograph, copied from Mrs. Cameron's original, of James Spedding—so fine that I know not whether I feel more pleasure or pain in looking at it. When you return to England, you shall see it somehow.

I have had a letter or two from Annie Ritchie, who is busy writing various Articles for Magazines. One concerning Miss Edgeworth in the Cornhill is pleasant reading. [250b] She tells me that Tennyson is at Aldworth (his Hampshire house, you know), and a notice in Athenæum or Academy tells that he is about to produce 'a Pastoral Drama' at one of the smaller Theatres! [251a]

You may have seen—but more probably have not seen—how Mr. Irving and Co. have brought out 'Much Ado' with all *éclat*.

It seems to me (but I believe it seems so every year) that our trees keep their leaves very long; I suppose because of no severe frosts or winds up to this time. And my garden still shows some Geranium, Salvia, Nasturtium, Great Convolvulus, and that grand African Marigold whose Colour is so comfortable to us Spanish-like Paddies. [251b] I have also a dear Oleander which even now has a score of blossoms on it, and touches the top of my little Greenhouse—having been sent me when 'haut comme ça,' as Marquis Somebody used to say in the days of Louis XIV. Don't you love the Oleander? So clean in its leaves and stem, as so beautiful in its flower; loving to stand in water, which it drinks up so fast. I rather worship mine.

Here is pretty matter to get Coutts to further on to Paris—to Mrs. Kemble in Paris. And I have written it all in my best MS. with a pen that has been held with its nib in water for more than a fortnight—Charles Keene's recipe for keeping Pens in condition—Oleander-like.

Please to make my Compliments to Mrs. Wister—my good wishes to the young Musician; [252a] and pray do you believe me your sincere as ever—in spite of his new name—

LITTLEGRANGE.

CIX.

[*Nov.*, 1882.]

MY DEAR MRS. KEMBLE:

You must be homeward-bound by this time, I think: but I hope my letter won't light upon you just when you are leaving Paris, or just arriving in London—perhaps about to see Mrs. Wister off to America from Liverpool! But you will know very well how to set my letter aside till some better opportunity. May Mrs. Wister fare well upon her Voyage over the Atlantic, and find all well when she reaches her home.

I have been again—twice or thrice—to Aldeburgh, when my contemporary old Beauty Mary Lynn was staying there; and pleasant Evenings enough we had, talking of other days, and she reading to me some of her Mudie Books, finishing with a nice little Supper, and some hot grog (for me) which I carried back to the fire, and *set on the carpet.* [252b] She read me (for one thing) 'Marjorie Fleming' from a Volume of Dr. Brown's Papers [253a]— read it as well as she could for laughing—'idiotically,' she said—but all the better to my mind. She had been very dismal all day, she said. Pray get some one to read you 'Marjorie'—which I say, because (as I found) it agrees with one best in that way. If only for dear Sir Walter's sake, who doated on the Child; and would not let his Twelfth Night be celebrated till she came through the Snow in a Sedan Chair, where (once in the warm Hall) he called all his Company down to see her nestling before he carried her upstairs in his arms. A very pretty picture. My old Mary said that Mr. Anstey's 'Vice Versa' made her and a friend, to whom she read it, laugh idiotically too: but I could not laugh over it alone, very clever as it is. And here is enough of me and Mary.

Devrient's Theory of Shakespeare's Sonnets (which you wrote me of) I cannot pretend to judge of: what he said of the Englishwomen, to whom the Imogens, Desdemonas, etc., were acceptable, seems to me well said. I named it to Aldis Wright in a letter, but what he thinks on the subject— surely no otherwise than Mrs. Kemble—I have not yet heard. My dear old Alfred's Pastoral troubles me a little—that he should have exposed himself to ridicule in his later days. Yet I feel sure that his aim is a noble one; and there was a good notice in the Academy [253b] saying there was much that was fine in the Play—nay, that a whole good Play might yet be made of it by some better Playwright's practical Skill.

And here is the end of my paper, before I have said something else that I had to say. But you have enough for the present from your ancient E. F.G.—who has been busy arranging some 'post mortem' papers.

CX.

WOODBRIDGE: *March* 6, [1883.]

MY DEAR MRS. KEMBLE,

I have asked more than one person for tidings of you, for the last two months: and only yesterday heard from M. Donne that he had seen you at the Address to which I shall direct this letter. I wrote to you about mid-November, desiring Coutts to forward my letter: in which I said that if you were in no mood to write during the time of Mrs. Wister's departure for America (which you had told me was to be November end) you were not to trouble yourself at all. Since which time I have really not known whether you had not gone off to America too. Anyhow, I thought better to wait till I had some token of your 'whereabout,' if nothing more. And now Mowbray tells me that much, and I will venture another Letter to you after so long an interval. You must always follow your own inclination as to answering me—not by any means make a 'Duty' of it.

As usual I have nothing to say of myself but what you have heard from me for years. Only that my (now one year old) friend Bronchitis has thus far done but little more than to keep me aware that he has not quitted me, nor even thinks of so doing. Nay, this very day, when the Snow which held off all winter is now coming down under stress of N.E. wind, I feel my friend stirring somewhat within.

Enough of that and of myself. Mowbray gives me a very good report of you—Absit Nemesis for my daring to write it!—And you have got back to something of our old London Quarters, which I always look to as better than the new. And do you go to even a Play, in the old Quarters also? Wright, who was with me at Christmas, was taken by Macmillan to see 'Much Ado,' and found, all except Scenery, etc. (which was too good) so bad that he vowed he would never go to see Sh. 'at any of your Courts' again. Irving without any Humour, Miss Terry with simply Animal Spirits, etc. However, Wright did intend once more to try—Comedy of Errors, at some theatre; but how he liked it—I may hear if he comes to me at Easter.

Now this is enough—is it not?—for a letter: but I am as always

Sincerely yours,

E. F.G.

CXI.

WOODBRIDGE: *April* 12, [1883.]

MY DEAR MRS. KEMBLE:

I do not think you will be sorry that more than a Moon has waxed and waned since last I wrote to you. For you have seen long enough how little I had to tell, and that nevertheless you were bound to answer. But all such Apologies are stale: you will believe, I hope, that I remain as I was in regard to you, as I shall believe that you are the same toward me.

Mowbray Donne has told me two months ago that he could not get over the Remembrance of last May; and that, acting on Body as well as Mind, aged him, I suppose, as you saw. Mowbray is one of the most loyal men toward Kinsman and Friend.

Now for my own little Budget of News. I got through those Sunless East winds well enough: better than I am feeling now they both work together. I think the Wind will rule till Midsummer: 'Enfin tant qu'il plaira à Dieu.' Aldis Wright was with me for Easter, and we went on our usual way, together or apart. Professor Norton had sent me his Carlyle-Emerson Correspondence, which we conned over together, and liked well on either side. Carlyle should not have said (and still less Norton printed) that Tennyson was a 'gloomy' Soul, nor Thackeray 'of inordinate Appetite,' neither of which sayings is true: nor written of Lord Houghton as a 'Robin Redbreast' of a man. I shall wait very patiently till Mudie sends me Jane Carlyle—where I am told there is a word of not unkindly toleration of me; which, if one be named at all, one may be thankful for. [257]

Here are two Questions to be submitted to Mrs. Kemble by Messrs. Aldis Wright and Littlegrange—viz., What she understands by—

(1.) 'The Raven himself is hoarse,' etc.

(2.) 'But this *eternal* Blazon must not be,' etc.

Mrs. Kemble (who *will* answer my letter) can tell me how she fares in health and well-being; yes, and if she has seen, or heard, anything of Alfred Tennyson, who is generally to be heard of in London at this time of year. And pray let Mrs. Kemble believe in the Writer of these poor lines as her ancient, and loyal, Subject

E. F.G.

'The raven himself is hoarse,' etc.

"Lady Macbeth compares the Messenger, hoarse for lack of Breath, to a raven whose croaking was held to be prophetic of Disaster. This we think the natural interpretation of the words, though it is rejected by some Commentators."—*Clark and Wright's Clarendon Press Shakespeare.*

"'Eternal Blazon' = revelation of Eternity. It may be, however, that Sh. uses 'eternal' for 'infernal' here, as in *Julius Cæsar* I. 2, 160: 'The eternal Devil'; and *Othello* IV. 2, 130: 'Some eternal villain.' 'Blazon' is an heraldic term, meaning Description of armorial bearings, * hence used for description generally; as in *Much Ado* II. 1, 307. The verb 'blazon' occurs in *Cymbeline* IV. 2, 170."—*Ibid.*

Thus have I written out in my very best hand: as I will take care to do in future; for I think it very bad manners to puzzle anyone—and especially a Lady—with that which is a trouble to read; and I really had no idea that I have been so guilty of doing so to Mrs. Kemble.

Also I beg leave to say that nothing in Mowbray's letter set me off writing again to Mrs. Kemble, except her Address, which I knew not till he gave it to me, and I remain her very humble obedient Servant,

THE LAIRD OF LITTLEGRANGE—

of which I enclose a side view done by a Woodbridge Artisan for his own amusement. So that Mrs. Kemble may be made acquainted with the '*habitat*' of the Flower—which is about to make an Omelette for its Sunday Dinner.

N.B.—The 'Raven' is not he that reports the news to Miladi M., but 'one of my fellows Who almost dead for breath, etc.'

* Not, as E. F.G. had thought, the Bearings themselves.

CXII.

[*May*, 1883.]

MY DEAR LADY,

I conclude (from what you wrote me in your last letter) that you are at Leamington by this time; and I will venture to ask a word of you before you go off to Switzerland, and I shall have to rely on Coutts & Co. for further Correspondence between us. I am not sure of your present Address, even should you be at Leamington—not sure—but yet I think my letter will find you—and, if it do not—why, then you will be saved the necessity of answering it.

I had written to Mowbray Donne to ask about himself and his Wife: and herewith I enclose his Answer—very sad, and very manly. You shall return it if you please; for I set some store by it.

Now I am reading—have almost finished—Jane Carlyle's Letters. I dare say you have already heard them more than enough discussed in London; and therefore I will only say that it is at any rate fine of old Carlyle to have laid himself so easily open to public Rebuke, though whether such Revelations are fit for Publicity is another question. At any rate, it seems to me that *half* her letters, and *all* his ejaculations of Remorse summed up in a Preface, would have done better. There is an Article by brave Mrs. Oliphant in this month's Contemporary Review [259] (or Magazine) well worth reading on the subject; with such a Challenge to Froude as might almost be actionable in Law. We must 'hear both sides,' and wait for the Volume which [is] to crown all his Labours in this Cause.

I think your Leamington Country is more in Leaf than ours 'down-East:' which only just begins to 'stand in a mist of green.' [260] By the by, I lately heard from Hallam Tennyson that all his Party were well enough; not having been to London this Spring because Alfred's Doctor had warned him against London Fogs, which suppress Perspiration, and bring up Gout. Which is the best piece of news in my Letter; and I am

Yours always and a Day
E. F.G.

P.S. I do not enclose Mowbray's letter, as I had intended to do, for fear of my own not finding you.

CXIII.

[*May,* 1883.]

MY DEAR LADY;

Stupid me! And now, after a little hunt, I find poor Mowbray's Letter, which I had made sure of having sent you. But I should not now send it if I did not implore you not to write in case you thought fit to return it; which indeed I did ask you to do; but now I would rather it remained with you, who will acknowledge all the true and brave in it as well as I—yes, it may be laid, if you please, even among those of your own which you tell me Mowbray's Father saved up for you. If you return it, let it be without a word of your own: and pray do not misunderstand me when I say that. You will hear of me (if Coutts be true) when you are among your

Mountains again; and, if you do hear of me, I know you will—for you must—reply.

At last some feeling of Spring—a month before Midsummer. And next week I am expecting my grave Friend Charles Keene, of Punch, to come here for a week—bringing with him his Bagpipes, and an ancient Viol, and a Book of Strathspeys and Madrigals; and our Archdeacon will come to meet him, and to talk over ancient Music and Books: and we shall all three drive out past the green hedges, and heaths with their furze in blossom—and I wish—yes, I do—that you were of the Party.

I love all Southey, and all that he does; and love that Correspondence of his with Caroline Bowles. We (Boy and I) have been reading an account of Zetland, which makes me thirst for 'The Pirate' again—tiresome, I know—more than half of it—but what a Vision it leaves behind! [261]

Now, Madam, you cannot pretend that you have to jump at my meaning through my MS. I am sure it is legible enough, and that I am ever yours

E. F.G.

You write just across the Address you date from; but I jump at that which I shall direct this Letter by.

CXIV.

WOODBRIDGE, *May* 27/83.

MY DEAR MRS. KEMBLE:

I feel minded to write you a word of Farewell before you start off for Switzerland: but I do not think it will be very welcome to you if, as usual, you feel bound to answer it on the Eve of your Departure. Why not let me hear from you when you are settled for a few days somewhere among your Mountains?

I was lately obliged to run to London on a disagreeable errand: which, however, got itself over soon after midday; when I got into a Cab to Chelsea, for the purpose of seeing Carlyle's Statue on the Embankment, and to take a last look at his old House in Cheyne Row. The Statue very good, I thought, though looking somewhat small for want of a good Background to set it off: but the old House! Shut up—neglected—'To Let'—was sad enough to me. I got back to Woodbridge before night. [263]

Since then I have had Charles Keene (who has not been well) staying with me here for ten days. He is a very good Guest, inasmuch as he entertains himself with Books, and Birds'-nests, and an ancient Viol which he has brought down here: as also a Bagpipe (his favourite instrument), only leaving the 'Bag' behind: he having to supply its functions from his own lungs. But he will leave me to-morrow or next day; and with June will come my two Nieces from Lowestoft: and then the Longest Day will come, and we shall begin declining toward Winter again, after so shortly escaping from it.

This very morning I receive The Diary of John Ward, Vicar of Stratford on Avon from 1648 to 1679—with some notices of W. S. which you know all about. And I am as ever

Sincerely yours
LITTLEGRANGE.

Is not this Letter legible enough?

Footnotes:

[3a] Mrs. Kemble's daughter, Frances Butler, was married to the Hon. and Rev. James Wentworth Leigh, now Dean of Hereford, 29th June 1871.

[3b] See 'Letters,' ii. 126.

[6] Fitzgerald's Lives of the Kembles was reviewed in the *Athenæum*, 12th August 1871, and the 'Memoirs of Mr. Harness,' 28th October.

[7] Macbeth, ii. 2, 21.

[9] In writing to Sir Frederick Pollock on November 17th, 1871, FitzGerald says:—

> 'The Game-dealer here telling me that he has some very good Pheasants, I have told him to send you a Brace—to go in company with Braces to Carlyle, and Mrs. Kemble. This will, you may think, necessitate your writing a Reply of Thanks before your usual time of writing: but don't do that:—only write to me now in case the Pheasants don't reach you; I know you will thank me for them, whether they reach you or not; and so you can defer writing so much till you happen next upon an idle moment which you may think as well devoted to me; you being the only man, except Donne, who cares to trouble himself with a gratuitous letter to one who really does not deserve it.
>
> 'Donne, you know, is pleased with Everybody, and with Everything that Anybody does for him. You must take his Praises of Woodbridge with this grain of Salt to season them. It may seem odd to you at first—but not perhaps on reflection—that I feel more—nervous, I may say—at the prospect of meeting with an old Friend, after all these years, than of any indifferent Acquaintance. I feel it the less with Donne, for the reason aforesaid—why should I not feel it with you who have given so many tokens since our last meeting that you are well willing to take me as I am? If one is, indeed, by Letter what one is in person.—I always tell Donne not to come out of his way here—he says he takes me in the course of a Visit to some East-Anglian kinsmen. Have you ever any such reason?—Well; if you have no better reason than that of really wishing to see me, for better or worse, in my home, come—some Spring or Summer day, when my Home at any rate is pleasant. This all sounds mock-modesty; but it is not; as I

can't read Books, Plays, Pictures, etc. and don't see People, I feel, when a Man comes, that I have all to ask and nothing to tell; and one doesn't like to make a Pump of a Friend.'

[10a] At the Royal Institution, on 'The Theatre in Shakespeare's Time.' The series consisted of six lectures, which were delivered from 20th January to 24th February 1872. On 18th February 1872, Mrs. Kemble wrote: 'My dear old friend Donne is lecturing on Shakespeare, and I have heard him these last two times. He is looking ill and feeble, and I should like to carry him off too, out of the reach of his too many and too heavy cares.'— 'Further Records,' ii. 253.

[10b] 27th February, 1872, for the recovery of the Prince of Wales.

[10c] Mr. Jenney, the owner of Bredfield House, where FitzGerald was born. See 'Letters,' i. 64.

[11] H. F. Chorley died 16th February 1872.

[13a] Perhaps Widmore, near Bromley. See 'Further Records,' ii. 253.

[13b] 'Old Kensington,' the first number of which appeared in the *Cornhill Magazine* for April 1872.

[15] He came May 18th, 1872, the day before Whitsunday.

[16a] F. T. came August 1st, 1872.

[16b] See 'Letters,' ii. 142-3.

[19a] Miss Harriet St. Leger.

[19b] April 14th, 1873. See 'Letters,' ii. 154.

[23a] Probably the piece beginning—

> 'On plante des pommiers ès bords
> Des cimitieres, près des morts, &c

Olivier Basselin ('Vaux-de-Vire,' ed Jacob, 1858, xv. p. 28)

On Oct 13th, 1879, FitzGerald wrote of a copy of Olivier (ed. Du Bois, 1821) which he had sent by me to Professor Cowell: "If Cowell does not care for Olivier—the dear Phantom!—pray do you keep him. Read a little piece—the two first Stanzas—beginning 'Dieu garde de deshonneur,' p. 184—quite beautiful to me; though not classed as Olivier's. Also 'Royne des Flours, &c,' p. 160. These are things that Béranger could not reach with all his Art; but Burns could without it."

[23b] De Damoyselle Anne de Marle (Marot, 'Cimetière,' xiv):—

'Lors sans viser au lieu dont elle vint,
Et desprisant la gloire que l'on a
En ce bas monde, icelle Anne ordonna,
Que son corps fust entre les pauures mys
En cette fosse. Or prions, chers amys,
Que l'ame soit entre les pauures mise,
Qui bien heureux sont chantez en l'Église.'

[25] On March 30, 1873, FitzGerald wrote to Sir Frederick Pollock:—

"At the beginning of this year I submitted to be Photo'ed
at last—for many Nieces, and a few old Friends—I must
think that you are an old Friend as well as a very kind and
constant one; and so I don't like not to send you what I
have sent others.—The Artist who took me, took (as he
always does) three several Views of one's Face: but the
third View (looking full-faced) got blurred by my blinking
at the Light: so only these two were reproduced—I
shouldn't know that either was meant for [me]: nor, I
think, would any one else, if not told: but the Truth-telling
Sun somehow did them; and as he acted so handsomely by
me, I take courage to distribute them to those who have a
regard for me, and will naturally like to have so favourable
a Version of one's Outward Aspect to remember one by.
I should not have sent them if they had been otherwise.
The up-looking one I call 'The Statesman,' quite ready to
be called to the Helm of Affairs: the Down-looking one I
call The Philosopher. Will you take which you like? And
when next old Spedding comes your way, give him the
other (he won't care which) with my Love. I only don't
write to him because my doing so would impose on his
Conscience an Answer—which would torment him for
some little while. I do not love him the less: and believe
all the while that he not the less regards me."

Again on May 5, he wrote: "I think I shall have a word about M[acready]
from Mrs. Kemble, with whom I have been corresponding a little since her
return to England. She has lately been staying with her Son in Law, Mr.
Leigh (?), at Stoneleigh Vicarage, near Kenilworth. In the Autumn she says
she will go to America, never to return to England. But I tell her she *will*
return. She is to sit for her Photo at my express desire, and I have given
her Instructions *how* to sit, derived from my own successful Experience.
One rule is to sit—in a dirty Shirt—(to avoid dangerous White) and
another is, not to sit on a Sunshiny Day: which we must leave to the
Young.

"By the by, I sent old Spedding my own lovely Photo (*the Statesman*) which he has acknowledged in Autograph. He tells me that he begins to 'smell Land' with his Bacon."

[28a] See 'Letters,' ii. 165-7.

[28b] See letter of April 22nd, 1873.

[30] Shakespeare, Ant. & Cl., v. 2, line 6:—

'Which shackles accidents, and bolts up change.'

[31] In his 'Half Hours with the Worst Authors' FitzGerald has transcribed 'Le Bon Pasteur,' which consists of five stanzas of eight lines each, beginning:—

'Bons habitans de ce Village,
Prêtez l'oreille un moment,' &c.

Each stanza ends:—

'Et le bon Dieu vous benira.'

He adds: 'One of the pleasantest remembrances of France is, having heard this sung to a Barrel-organ, and chorus'd by the Hearers (who had bought the Song-books) one fine Evening on the Paris Boulevards, June: 1830.'

[34a] Haydon entered these verses in his Diary for May, 1846: 'The struggle is severe, for myself I care not, but for her so dear to me I feel. It presses on her mind, and in a moment of pain, she wrote the following simple bit of feeling to Frederick, who is in South America, on Board *The Grecian.*' There are seven stanzas in the original, but FitzGerald has omitted in his transcript the third and fourth and slightly altered one or two of the lines. He called them 'A poor Mother's Verses.'

[34b] See 'Letters,' ii. 280.

[37] Burns, quoted from memory as usual. See Globe Edition, p. 214; ed. Cunningham, iv. 293.

[38] Greville Sartoris was killed by a fall from his horse, not in the hunting-field, 23 Oct. 1873.

[39] 'Rage' in the original. See Tales of the Hall, Book XII. Sir Owen Dale.

[40] Quoting from Peacock's 'Headlong Hall':—

'Nature had but little clay
Like that of which she moulded him.'

See 'Letters,' i. 75, note.

[42] 18 April 1874. Professor Hiram Corson endeavoured to maintain the correctness of the reading of the Folios in Antony and Cleopatra, v. 2. 86-88:

> 'For his Bounty,
> There was no winter in 't. An *Anthony* it was,
> That grew the more by reaping.'

Spedding admirably defended Theobald's certain emendation of 'autumn' for 'Anthony.'

[43] These lines are not to be found in Crabbe, so far as I can ascertain, but they appear to be a transformation of two which occur in the Parish Register, Part II., in the story of Phebe Dawson (Works, ii. 183):

> 'Friend of distress! The mourner feels thy aid;
> She cannot pay thee, but thou wilt be paid.'

They had taken possession of FitzGerald's memory in their present shape, for in a letter to me, dated 5 Nov. 1877, speaking of the poet's son, who was Vicar of Bredfield, he says: "It is now just twenty years since the Brave old Boy was laid in Bredfield Churchyard. Two of his Father's Lines might make Epitaph for some good soul:—

> 'Friend of the Poor, the Wretched, the Betray'd;
> They cannot pay thee—but thou shalt be paid.'

Pas mal ça, eh!"

[45a] In a letter to me dated October 29th, 1871, FitzGerald says:—

> "A suggestion that casually fell from old Spedding's lips (I forget how long ago) occurred to me the other day. Instead of
>
> 'Do such business as the bitter day,'

read 'better day'—a certain Emendation, I think. I hope you take Spedding into your Counsel; he might be induced to look over one Play at a time though he might shrink from all in a Body; and I scarce ever heard him conning a page of Shakespeare but he suggested something which was an improvement—on Shakespeare himself, if not on his Editors—though don't [tell] Spedding that I say so, for God's sake."

[45b] In 'Notes and Queries,' April 18th, 1874.

[48a] Lord Hertford

[48b] Frank Carr Beard, the friend and medical adviser of Dickens and Wilkie Collins.

[49a] See Lockhart's 'Life of Scott,' vii. 394. 'About half-past one, P.M., on the 21st of September, [1832], Sir Walter breathed his last, in the presence of all his children. It was a beautiful day—so warm that every window was wide open, and so perfectly still, that the sound of all others most delicious to his ear, the gentle ripple of the Tweed over its pebbles, was distinctly audible as we knelt around the bed, and his eldest son kissed and closed his eyes.'

[49b] Dryburgh.

[49c] The North West Passage. The 'Old Sea Captain' was Trelawny.

[50a] See 'Letters,' ii. 173-4.

[50b] E. F. S. Pigott.

[52] See 'Letters,' ii. 172.

[53a] Not *Macmillan*, but *Cornhill Magazine*, Dec. 1863, 'On the Stage.' See Letter of 24 Aug. 1875.

[53b] "Pasta, the great lyric tragedian, who, Mrs. Siddons said, was capable of giving her lessons, replied to the observation, 'Vous avez dû beaucoup étudier l'antique.' 'Je l'ai beaucoup senti.'"—From Mrs. Kemble's article 'On the Stage' ('Cornhill,' 1863), reprinted as an Introduction to her Notes upon some of Shakespeare's Plays.

[53c] 'Causeries du Lundi,' xiv. 234.

[53d] Lettre de Viard a M. Walpole, in 'Lettres de Madame du Deffand,' iv. 178 (Paris, 1824). FitzGerald probably read it in Ste. Beuve, 'Causeries du Lundi,' i. 405.

[54] Cedars, not yew. See Memoirs of Chorley, ii. 240.

[55] In Tales of the Hall, Book XI. ('Works,' vi. 284), quoted from memory.

[56] Virgil, Æn. vi. 127.

[57a] Referring to the well-known print of 'Remarkable Characters who were at Tunbridge Wells with Richardson in 1748.'

[57b] James Spedding.

[59a] In the original draft of Tales of the Hall, Book VI.

[59b] See Memoirs of Chateaubriand, written by himself, Eng. trans. 1849 p. 123. At the Château of Combourg in Brittany, 'When supper was over, and the party of four had removed from the table to the chimney, my mother would throw herself, with a sigh, upon an old cotton-covered sofa,

and near her was placed a little stand with a light. I sat down by the fire with Lucile; the servants removed the supper-things, and retired. My father then began to walk up and down, and never ceased until his bedtime. He wore a kind of white woollen gown, or rather cloak, such as I have never seen with anyone else. His head, partly bald, was covered with a large white cap, which stood bolt upright. When, in the course of his walk, he got to a distance from the fire, the vast apartment was so ill-lighted by a single candle that he could be no longer seen, he could still be heard marching about in the dark, however, and presently returned slowly towards the light, and emerged by degrees from obscurity, looking like a spectre, with his white robe and cap, and his tall, thin figure.'

[64a] 'The Mighty Magician' and 'Such Stuff as Dreams are made of.'

[64b] See Winter's Tale, iv. 4, 118-120.

[65] 'Euphranor.'

[67] See 'Letters,' ii. 180.

[68] Sir Arthur Helps died March 7th, 1875.

[69] The Passage of Carlyle to which FitzGerald refers is perhaps in 'Anti-Dryasdust,' in the Introduction to Cromwell's Letters and Speeches. 'By very nature it is a labyrinth and chaos, this that we call Human History; an *abatis* of trees and brushwood, a world-wide jungle, at once growing and dying. Under the green foliage and blossoming fruit-trees of To-day, there lie, rotting slower or faster, the forests of all other Years and Days. Some have rotted fast, plants of annual growth, and are long since quite gone to inorganic mould; others are like the aloe, growths that last a thousand or three thousand years.' Ste. Beuve, in his 'Nouveaux Lundis' (iv. 295), has a similar remark: 'Pour un petit nombre d'arbres qui s'élèvent de quelques pieds au-dessus de terre et qui s'aperçoivent de loin, il y a partout, en littérature, de cet humus et de ce détrius végétal, de ces feuilles accumulées et entassées qu'on ne distingue pas, si l'on ne se baisse.' At the end of his copy FitzGerald has referred to this as 'Carlyle's Peat.'

[71] In The Gamester. See 'Macready's Reminiscences,' i. 54-57.

[72a] In Rowe's Tamerlane. See 'Macready's Reminiscences,' i. 202.

[72b] Probably the English Tragedy, which was finished in October 1838. See 'Records of Later Days,' ii. 168.

[74] In the *Transactions of the New Shakspere Society* for 1875-76. The surviving editor of the 'Cambridge Shakspeare' does not at all feel that Spedding's criticism 'smashed' the theory which was only put forward as a tentative solution of a perhaps insoluble problem.

[75a] See 'Letters,' ii. 177.

[75b] See 'Letters,' ii. 198, 228, and Boswell's 'Johnson' (ed. Birkbeck Hill), iv. 193.

[77] FitzGerald wrote to me about the same time:

> "Spedding has (you know) a delicious little Paper about the Merchant of Venice in July *Fraser.*—but I think he is wrong in subordinating Shylock to the Comedy Part. If that were meant to be so, Williams ['the divine Williams,' as some Frenchman called Shakespeare] miscalculated, throwing so much of his very finest writing into the Jew's Mouth, the downright human Nature of which makes all the Love-Story Child's play, though very beautiful Child's play indeed."

[78] 'On the Stage,' in the *Cornhill Magazine* for December 1863 Reprinted as an Introduction to Mrs. Kemble's 'Notes upon some of Shakespeare's Plays.'

[79] See his 'Life and Letters,' p. 46.

[80] In the *Cornhill Magazine* for July 1875, The Merchant of Venice at the Prince of Wales's Theatre.

[82a] 'The Enterprising Impresario' by Walter Maynard (Thomas Willert Beale), 1867, pp 273-4.

[82b] Beginning, 'A spirit haunts the year's last hours.' It first appeared in the poems of 1830, p. 67, and is now included in Tennyson's Collected Works. See 'Letters,' ii. 256.

[82c] By Sir Gilbert Elliot, father of the first Lord Minto. The query appeared 25 Sept. 1875 ('N. & Q.' 5th Series, iv. 247), and two answers are given at p. 397, but not by E. F.G.

[83] See 'Letters,' ii. 185.

[84] The *Atlantic Monthly* for August, September, and October 1875.

[85a] *Atlantic Monthly*, August 1875, p. 167, by T. S. Perry.

[85b] *Ibid.*, p. 240.

[86] From Oct. 30 to Nov. 4.

[87a] The Trial of Queen Katharine in *Henry VIII.* Charles Kemble acted Cromwell.

[87b] *Atlantic Monthly*, August 1875, p. 165.

[88a] 'The Exile,' quoted from memory.

[88b] See letter of August 24, 1875.

[89] *Atlantic Monthly*, August 1875, p. 156.

[90a] Thomas Griffiths Wainewright. De Quincey's account of him is in his essay on Charles Lamb ('Works,' ed. 1862, viii. 146). His career was the subject of a story by Dickens, called 'Hunted Down.'

[90b] Minnie Thackeray (Mrs. Leslie Stephen) died Nov. 28.

[91] About the same time he wrote to me:—

> 'A dozen years ago I entreated Annie Thackeray, Smith & Elder, &c., to bring out a Volume of Thackeray's better Drawings. Of course they wouldn't—now Windus and Chatto have, you know, brought out a Volume of his inferior: and now Annie T. S. & E. prepare a Volume— when it is not so certain to pay, at any rate, as when W. M. T. was the Hero of the Day. However, I send them all I have: pretty confident they will select the worst; of course, for my own part, I would rather have any other than copies of what I have: but I should like the World to acknowledge he could do something beside the ugly and ridiculous. Annie T. sent me the enclosed Specimen: very careless, but full of Character. I can see W. M. T. drawing it as he was telling one about his Scotch Trip. That disputatious Scotchman in the second Row with Spectacles, and—teeth. You may know some who will be amused at this:—but send it back, please: no occasion to write beside.'

[92] When I was preparing the first edition of FitzGerald's Letters I wrote to Mrs. Kemble for permission to quote the passage from her Gossip which is here referred to. She replied (11 Dec. 1883):—

> 'I have no objection whatever to your quoting what I said of Edward Fitzgerald in the *Atlantic Monthly*, but I suppose you know that it was omitted from Bentley's publication of my book at Edward's *own desire*. He did not certainly knock me on the head with Dr. Johnson's sledge-hammer, but he did make me feel painfully that I had been guilty of the impertinence of praising.'

I did not then avail myself of the permission so readily granted, but I venture to do so now, in the belief that the publicity from which his sensitive nature shrank during his lifetime may now without impropriety be given to what was written in all sincerity by one of his oldest and most intimate friends. It was Mrs. Kemble who described him as 'an eccentric man of genius, who took more pains to avoid fame than others do to seek it,' and this description is fully borne out by the account she gave of him in the offending passage which follows:—

"That Mrs. Fitzgerald is among the most vivid memories of my girlish days. She and her husband were kind and intimate friends of my father and mother. He was a most amiable and genial Irish gentleman, with considerable property in Ireland and Suffolk, and a fine house in Portland Place, and had married his cousin, a very handsome, clever, and eccentric woman. I remember she always wore a bracelet of his hair, on the massive clasp of which were engraved the words, '*Stesso sangue, stessa sorte.*' I also remember, as a feature of sundry dinners at their house, the first gold dessert and table ornaments that I ever saw, the magnificence of which made a great impression upon me; though I also remember their being replaced, upon Mrs. Fitzgerald's wearying of them, by a set of ground glass and dead and burnished silver, so exquisite that the splendid gold service was pronounced infinitely less tasteful and beautiful. One member of her family— her son Edward Fitzgerald—has remained my friend till this day. His parents and mine are dead. Of his brothers and sisters I retain no knowledge, but with him I still keep up an affectionate and to me most valuable and interesting correspondence. He was distinguished from the rest of his family, and indeed from most people, by the possession of very rare intellectual and artistic gifts. A poet, a painter, a musician, an admirable scholar and writer, if he had not shunned notoriety as sedulously as most people seek it, he would have achieved a foremost place among the eminent men of his day, and left a name second to that of very few of his contemporaries. His life was spent in literary leisure, or literary labours of love of singular excellence, which he never cared to publish beyond the circle of his intimate friends: Euphranor, Polonius, collections of dialogues full of keen wisdom, fine observation, and profound thought; sterling philosophy written in the purest, simplest, and raciest English; noble translations, or rather free adaptations of Calderon's two finest dramas, The Wonderful Magician and Life's a Dream, and a splendid paraphrase of the

Agamemnon of Æschylus, which fills its reader with regret that he should not have *Englished* the whole of the great trilogy with the same severe sublimity. In America this gentleman is better known by his translation or adaptation (how much more of it is his own than the author's I should like to know if I were Irish) of Omar Khayyám, the astronomer-poet of Persia. Archbishop Trench, in his volume on the life and genius of Calderon, frequently refers to Mr. Fitzgerald's translations, and himself gives a version of Life's a Dream, the excellence of which falls short, however, of his friend's finer dramatic poem bearing the same name, though he has gallantly attacked the difficulty of rendering the Spanish in English verse. While these were Edward Fitzgerald's studies and pursuits, he led a curious life of almost entire estrangement from society, preferring the companionship of the rough sailors and fishermen of the Suffolk coast to that of lettered folk. He lived with them in the most friendly intimacy, helping them in their sea ventures, and cruising about with one, an especially fine sample of his sort, in a small fishing-smack which Edward Fitzgerald's bounty had set afloat, and in which the translator of Calderon and Æschylus passed his time, better pleased with the fellowship and intercourse of the captain and crew of his small fishing craft than with that of more educated and sophisticated humanity. He and his brothers were school-fellows of my eldest brother under Dr. Malkin, the master of the grammar school of Bury St. Edmunds."

[94] Mrs. Kemble's letter was written with a typewriter (see 'Further Records,' i. 198, 240, 247). It was given by FitzGerald to Mr. F. Spalding, now of the Colchester Museum, through whose kindness I am enabled to quote it:—

'YORK FARM, BRANCHTOWN.
'*Tuesday, Dec.* 14. 1875.

'MY DEAR EDWARD FITZGERALD,

'I have got a printing-machine and am going to try and write to you upon it and see if it will suit your eyes better than my scrawl of handwriting. Thank you for the Photographs and the line of music; I know that old bit of tune, it seems to me. I think Mr. Irving's face more like Young's than my Father's. Tom Taylor, years ago, told me that Miss Ellen Terry would be a consummate comic actress. Portia should never be without some one to set her before the Public. She is my model woman.'

[97a] See 'Letters,' ii. 192

[97b] See the *Athenæum* for Jan. 1, 15, 22, 29, 1876.

[100] In her 'Further Records,' i. 250, Mrs. Kemble wrote, March 11th, 1876:—

> 'Last week my old friend Edward Fitzgerald (Omar Kyam, you know), sent me a beautiful miniature of my mother, which his mother—her intimate friend—had kept till her death, and which had been painted for Mrs. Fitzgerald. It is a full-length figure, very beautifully painted, and very like my mother. Almost immediately after receiving this from England, my friend Mr. Horace Furness came out to see me. He is a great collector of books and prints, and brought me an old engraving of my mother in the character of Urania, which a great many years ago I remember to have seen, and which was undoubtedly the original of Mrs. Fitzgerald's miniature. I thought the concidence of their both reaching me at the same time curious.'

[105] On July 22nd, 1880, he wrote to me:—"I am still reading her! And could make a pretty Introduction to her; but Press-work is hard to me now, and nobody would care for what I should do, when done. Mrs. Edwards has found me a good Photo of 'nos pauvres Rochers,' a straggling old Château, with (I suppose) the Chapel which her old 'Bien Bon' Uncle built in 1671—while she was talking to her Gardener Pilois and reading Montaigne, Molière, Pascal, *or* Cleopatra, among the trees she had planted. Bless her! I should like to have made Lamb like her, in spite of his anti-gallican Obstinacy."

[106] Mrs. Charles Donne, daughter of John Mitchell Kemble, died April 15th, 1876.

[107] First acted April 18th, 1876.

[108a] See 'Letters,' ii. 293.

[108b] See 'Letters,' ii. 198.

[109a] *Atlantic Monthly*, June 1876, p. 719.

[109b] Which opened May 10th, 1876.

[110] In one of his Common Place Books FitzGerald has entered from the *Monthly Mirror* for 1807 the following passage of Rousseau on Stage Scenery—'Ils font, pour épouventer, un Fracas de Decorations sans Effet. Sur la scene même il ne faut pas tout dire à la Vue: mais ébranler l'Imagmation.'

[111] For April and May 1876: 'The Latest Theory about Bacon.'

[113a] See letter of October 4th, 1875

[113b] See 'Letters,' ii. 202-205.

[113c] This card is now in my possession, 'Mr. Alfred Tennyson. Farringford.' On it is written in pencil, "Dear old Fitz—I am passing thro' and will call again. [The last three words are crossed out and 'am here' is written over them]. A.T." FitzGerald enclosed it to Thompson (Master of Trinity) and wrote on the back, 'P.S. Since writing, this card was sent in: the Writer followed with his Son: and here we all are as if twenty years had not passed since we met.'

[114a] About the same time he wrote to me:—"Tennyson came here suddenly ten days ago—with his Son Hallam, whom I liked much. It was a Relief to find a Young Gentleman not calling his Father 'The Governor' but even—'Papa,' and tending him so carefully in all ways. And nothing of 'awfully jolly,' etc. I put them up at the Inn—Bull—as my own House was in a sort of Interregnum of Painting, within and without: and I knew they would be well provided at 'John Grout's'—as they were. Tennyson said he had not found such Dinners at Grand Hotels, etc. And John (though a Friend of Princes of all Nations—Russian, French, Italian, etc.—who come to buy Horse flesh) was gratified at the Praise: though he said to me 'Pray, Sir, what is the name of the Gentleman?'"

[114b] On September 11th, 1877, he wrote to me: 'You ought to have Hugo's French Shakespeare: it is not wonderful to see how well a German Translation thrives:—but French Prose—no doubt better than French Verse. When I was looking over King John the other day I knew that Napoleon would have owned it as the thing he craved for in the Theatre: as also the other Historical Plays:—not Love of which one is sick: but the Business of Men. He said this at St. Helena, or elsewhere.'

[115] It was in 1867. See 'Letters,' ii. 90, 94.

[116] Life, vi. 215. Letter to Lockhart, January 15th, 1826.

[117a] These expressions must not be looked for in the Decameron, as 'emendato secondo l'ordine del Sacro Concilio di Trento.'

[117b] See 'Letters,' ii. 203. In a letter to me dated November 4th, 1876, he says:—

"I have taken refuge from the Eastern Question in Boccaccio, just as the 'piacevoli Donne' who tell the Stories escaped from the Plague. I suppose one must read this in Italian as my dear Don in Spanish: the Language of each fitting the Subject 'like a Glove.' But there is nothing to come up to the Don and his Man."

[118] Book XVIII., vol. vii. p. 188.

[119a] See 'Letters,' ii. 208.

[119b] Gillies' Memoirs of a Literary Veteran. See Letters, ii. 197, 199.

[120a] An Ode for the Fourth of July, 1876.

[120b] Mr. Wade, author of *The Jew of Aragon*, which failed. Mrs. Kemble says (*Atlantic Monthly*, December 1876, p. 707):—

> "I was perfectly miserable when the curtain fell, and the poor young author, as pale as a ghost, came forward to meet my father at the side scene, and bravely holding out his hand to him said, 'Never mind, Mr. Kemble, I'll do better another time.'"

[120c] Francisco Javier Elio, a Spanish General, was executed in 1822 for his seventies against the liberals dining the reactionary period 1814-1820.

[122a] *Atlantic Monthly*, February 1877, p. 222.

[122b] Holbrook, near Ipswich. That she had also some of the family humour is evident from what she wrote to Mr. Crabbe of her brother's early life. 'As regards spiritual advantages out of the house he had none; for our Pastor was one of the old sort, with a jolly red nose caused by good cheer. He used to lay his Hat and Whip on the Communion Table and gabble over the service, running down the Pulpit Stairs not to lose the opportunity of being invited to a good dinner at the Hall.' It was with reference to his sister's husband that FitzGerald in conversation with Tennyson used the expression 'A Mr. Wilkinson, a clergyman.'

'Why, Fitz,' said Tennyson, 'that's a verse, and a very bad one too.' And they would afterwards humorously contend for the authorship of the worst line in the English language.

[123] *Atlantic Monthly*, February 1877, pp. 210, 211, and pp. 220, 221.

[124a] See note to Letter of Dec. 29*th* 1875.

[124b] For November 1875, in an article called 'The Judgment of Paris,' p. 400.

[125a] See 'Letters,' ii. 217. This is in my possession.

[125b] It came to an end in April 1877. In a letter to Miss St. Leger, December 31st, 1876 ('Further Records,' ii. 33), Mrs. Kemble says, 'You ask me how I mean to carry on the publication of my articles in the *Atlantic Magazine* when I leave America; but I do not intend to carry them on. The editor proposed to me to do so, but I thought it would entail so much trouble and uncertainty in the transmission of manuscript and proofs, that it would be better to break off when I came to Europe. The editor will have manuscript enough for the February, March, and April numbers when I come away, and with those I think the series must close. As there is no narrative or sequence of events involved in the publication, it can, of course, be stopped at any moment; a story without an end can end anywhere.'

[126] See letter of December 29th, 1875.

[127a] 15, Connaught Square. See 'Further Records,' ii. 42, etc.

[127b] Valentia Donne marred the Rev. R. F. Smith, minor Canon of Southwell, May 24th, 1877.

[131a] 'We might say in a short word, which means a long matter, that your Shakespeare fashions his characters from the heart outwards, your Scott fashions them from the skin inwards, never getting near the heart of them.'—Carlyle, 'Miscellanies,' vi. 69 (ed. 1869), 'Sir Walter Scott'

[131b] Procter, 'Autobiographical Fragments,' p. 154.

[134a] February 9th, 1878.

[134b] It was not in the *Fortnightly* but in the *Nineteenth Century.*

[134c] This portrait is in my possession. FitzGerald fastened it in a copy of the 'Poems chiefly Lyrical' (1830) which he gave me bound up with the 'Poems' of 1833. He wrote underneath, 'Done in a Steamboat from Gravesend to London, Jan: 1842.'

[135a] Criticisms and Elucidations of Catullus by H. A. J. Munro.

[135b] See 'Letters,' ii. 233, 235, 236, 238, 239.

[136] See 'Letters,' ii. 247.

[138a] See 'Letters,' ii. 243.

[138b] See 'Letters,' ii. 248.

[145] See 'Letters,' ii. 265.

[146] II. 166 (ed. 1826).

[149] John Purcell FitzGerald died at Boulge, May 4th, 1879.

[151a] See letter of May 5th, 1877.

[151b] In a letter to me dated May 7th, 1879, he says:—

> 'I see by Athenæum that Charles Tennyson (Turner) is dead. *Now* people will begin to talk of his beautiful Sonnets: small, but original, things, as well as beautiful. Especially after that somewhat absurd Sale of the Brothers' early Editions.'

[152] Gay, *The Beggar's Opera*, Act III, Air 57.

[153] Professor Skeat's Inaugural Lecture, in *Macmillan's Magazine* for February 1879, pp. 304-313.

[154] Mrs. Sartoris, Mrs. Kemble's sister, died August 4, 1879. See 'Further Records,' ii. 277.

[155] Edwin Edwards, who died September 15. See 'Letters,' ii. 277.

[157] In a letter to me of September 29 1879, he says, "My object in going to London is, to see poor Mrs. Edwards, who writes me that she has much collapsed in strength (no wonder!) after the Trial she endured for near three years more or less, and, you know, a very hard light for the last year . . .

"Besides her, Mrs. Kemble, who has lately lost her Sister, and returned from Switzerland to London just at a time when most of her Friends are out of it—*she* wants to see me, an old Friend of hers and her Family's, whom she has not seen for more than twenty years. So I do hope to do my 'petit possible' to solace both these poor Ladies at the same time."

[158] On September 11 he wrote to me, 'Ah, pleasant Dunwich Days! I should never know a better Boy than Edwards, nor a braver little Wife than her, were I to live six times as long as I am like to do.'

[160] See letter of October 4, 1875.

[161] Mrs. Leigh's son, Pierce Butler, was born on Sunday, November 2, 1879.

[162] See 'Letters,' ii. 326.

[163a] Mrs. Kemble appears to have adopted this suggestion. In her 'Records of a Girlhood,' ii. 41, she says of Sir Thomas Lawrence, 'He came repeatedly to consult with my mother about the disputed point of my dress,

and gave his sanction to her decision upon it. The first dress of Belvidera [in *Venice Preserved*], I remember, was a point of nice discussion between them. . . . I was allowed (not, however, without serious demur on the part of Lawrence) to cover my head with a black hat and white feather.'

[163b] William Mason.

[166] November 10, 1879.

[168] Mrs. De Soyres died at Exeter, December 11, 1879.

[169] Played at St. James's Theatre, December 18, 1879.

[171] 'The Duke's Children.'

[173] Probably the 'Records of Later Life,' published in 1882.

[174] On 1st February 1880, FitzGerald wrote to me:—"Do you know what 'Stub Iron' is? (I do), and what 'Heel-taps' derives from, which Mrs. Kemble asks, and I cannot tell her." This is probably the query referred to.

[175] Beginning 'As men may children at their sports behold!'—Tales of the Hall, book xxi., at the end of 'Smugglers and Poachers.'

[176] In the *Cornhill Magazine*, March 1880, 'The Story of the Merchant of Venice.'

[179] 'An Eye-witness of John Kemble,' by Sir Theodore Martin. The eye-witness is Tieck.

[180a] This letter was written on a Tuesday, and April 6 was a Tuesday in 1880. Moreover, in 1880, at Easter, Donne's house was in quarantine. FitzGerald probably had the advanced sheets of the *Atlantic Monthly* for May from Professor Norton as early as the beginning of April.

[180b] The *Atlantic Monthly* for May 1880, contained an article by Mr. G. E. Woodberry on Crabbe, 'A Neglected Poet.' See letter to Professor Norton, May 1, 1880, in 'Letters,' ii. 281.

[181a] No. 39, where FitzGerald's father and mother lived. See 'Records of a Girlhood,' iii. 28.

[181b] See 'Letters,' ii. 138.

[183a] It was Queen Catharine. When Mrs. Siddons called upon Johnson in 1783, he "particularly asked her which of Shakespeare's characters she was most pleased with. Upon her answering that she thought the character of Queen Catharine, in *Henry the Eighth*, the most natural:—'I think so too, Madam, (said he;) and when ever you perform it, I will once more hobble out to the theatre myself.'"—Boswell's 'Life of Johnson' (ed. Birkbeck Hill), iv. 242.

[183b] See letters of February and December 1881.

[184a] See 'Letters,' ii. 244, 249.

[184b] On June 30, 1880, he wrote to me, 'Half her Beauty is the liquid melodiousness of her language—all unpremeditated as a Blackbird's.'

[186] See letter of May 5, 1877.

[187] In a letter to me of the same date he wrote: 'Last night when Miss Tox was just coming, like a good Soul, to ask about the ruined Dombey, we heard a Splash of Rain, and I had the Book shut up, and sat listening to the Shower by myself—till it blew over, I am sorry to say, and no more of the sort all night. But we are thankful for that small mercy.

'I am reading through my Sévigné again—welcome as the flowers of May.'

[188a] On June 9, 1879, FitzGerald wrote to me: "I was from Tuesday to Saturday last in Norfolk with my old Bredfield Party—George, not very well: and, as he has not written to tell me he is better, I am rather anxious. You should know him; and his Country: which is still the old Country which we have lost here; small enclosures, with hedgeway timber: green gipsey drift-ways: and Crome Cottage and Farmhouse of that beautiful yellow 'Claylump' with red pantile roof'd—not the d---d Brick and Slate of these parts."

[188b] See 'Letters,' ii. 290.

[190] See letter of Madame de Sévigné to Madame de Grignan, June 15, 1689.

[191] In one of FitzGerald's Common Place Books he gives the story thus: "When Chancellor Cheverny went home in his Old Age and for the last time, 'Messieurs' (dit-il aux Gentilshommes du Canton accourus pour le saluer), 'Je ressemble au bon Lièvre qui vient mourir au Gîte.'"

[192a] Tom Taylor died July 12, 1880.

[192b] On July 16 FitzGerald wrote to me: 'Not being assured that you were back from Revision, I wrote yesterday to Cowell asking him—and you, when returned—to call on Professor Goodwin, of American Cambridge, who goes to-morrow to your Cambridge—to see—if not to stay with—Mr. Jebb. Mr. Goodwin proposed to give me a look here before he went to Cambridge: but I told him I could not bear the thought of his coming all this way for such a purpose. I think you can witness that I do not wish even old English Friends to take me except on their way elsewhere: and for an American Gentleman! It is not affectation to say that any such proposal worried me. So what must I do but ask him to be sure to see Messrs. Wright and Cowell when he got to Cambridge: and spend

part of one of his days there in going to Bury, and (even if he cared not for the Abbey with its Abbot Samson and Jocelyn) to sit with a Bottle of light wine at the Angel window, face to face with that lovely Abbey gate. Perhaps Cowell, I said, might go over with him—knowing and loving Gothic—that was a liberty for me to take with Cowell, but he need not go—I did not hint at you. I suppose I muddled it all. But do show the American Gentleman some civilities, to make amends for the disrespect which you and Cowell told me of in April.'

[193] The defeat of General Burrows by Ayoub Khan, announced in the House of Commons, July 28, 1880. On July 29 further telegrams reported that General Burrows and other officers had arrived at Candahar after the defeat.

[194] The date should be September 19, which was a Sunday in 1880. Full moon was on September 18.

[197] In her 'Further Records,' i. 295, Mrs. Kemble says, 'Russia leather, you know, is almost an element of the atmosphere of my rooms, as all the shades of violet and purple are of their colouring, so that my familiar friends associate the two with their notions of my habitat.'

[198] See 'Life of Crabbe,' p. 262.

[200] See 'Letters,' ii. 295.

[201a] On 'The Story of the Merchant of Venice' in the *Cornhill Magazine* for March 1880.

[201b] 'Ballads and other Poems,' 1880.

[202] *Kelter*, condition, order. Forby's 'Vocabulary of East Anglia.'

[203a] See 'Letters,' ii. 110

[203b] 'Medusa and other Tales' (1868), republished in 1880 with a preface by her daughter, Mrs. Gordon.

[205] Full moon February 14th.

[206a] Acted at the Lyceum, January 3rd, 1881.

[206b] For February 1881.

[210] See letters of April 23rd, 1880, and December 1881.

[211a] See 'Letters,' ii. 180, 320.

[211b] Printed in 'Letters,' ii. 298-301.

[214] Partly printed in 'Letters,' ii. 305-7.

[216a] Printed in 'Letters,' ii. 310-312.

[216b] April 17th was Easter Day in 1881.

[217] Madame de Sévigné writes from Chaulnes, April 17th, 1689, 'A peine le vert veut-il montrer le nez; pas un rossignol encore; enfin, l'hiver le 17 d'Avril.'

[218] In *Macmillan's Magazine* for April 1881.

[219] Partly printed in 'Letters,' ii. 313.

[221] Partly printed in 'Letters,' ii. 312.

[227a] On Madame de Sévigné.

[227b] Published in 1882 as 'Records of Later Life.'

[227c] See letter of August 24th, 1875.

[230] Partly printed in 'Letters,' ii. 320-1.

[231] The correct date is 1794-1805.

[233] 'Evenings with a Reviewer.' The Reviewer was Macaulay, and the review the Essay on Bacon.

[234a] At Boulge.

[234b] He was in London from February 17th to February 20th.

[236] See 'Letters,' ii. 324-6.

[237a] Full moon April 3rd, 1882.

[237b] 'Thomas Carlyle. The Man and His Books.' By W. H. Wylie. 1881, p. 363.

[241a] On May 7 FitzGerald wrote to me from Lowestoft:

> "I too am taking some medicine, which, whatever effect it has on me, leaves an indelible mark on Mahogany: for (of course) I spilled a lot on my Landlady's Chiffonier, and found her this morning rubbing at the 'damned Spot' with Turpentine, and in vain."

And two days later:

> "I was to have gone home to-day: but Worthington wishes me to stay, at any rate, till the week's end, by which time he thinks to remove what he calls 'a Crepitation' in one lung, by help of the Medicine which proved its power on the mahogany. Yesterday came a Cabinet-maker, who was

for more than half an hour employed in returning that to its 'sound and pristine health,' or such as I hope my Landlady will be satisfied with."

[241b] Serjeant Ballantine's 'Experiences of a Barrister's Life' appeared in March 1882.

[241c] Full moon was June 1st, 1882.

[243a] W. B. Donne died June 20th, 1882.

[243b] This letter is in my possession, and as it indicates what Mr. Froude's plan originally was, though he afterwards modified it, I have thought it worth while to give it in full.

'5 ONSLOW GARDENS, S.W.
'*May* 19.

'DEAR MR. FITZGERALD,

'Certainly you are no stranger to me. I have heard so often from Carlyle, and I have read so much in his letters, about your exertions, and about your entertainment of him at various times, that I can hardly persuade myself that I never saw you.

'The letters you speak of must be very interesting, and I would ask you to let me see them if I thought that they were likely to be of use to me; but the subject with which I have to deal is so vast that I am obliged to limit myself, and so intricate that I am glad to be able to limit myself. I shall do what Carlyle desired me to do, *i.e.* edit the collection of his wife's letters, which he himself prepared for publication.

'This gift or bequest of his governs the rest of my work. What I have already done is an introduction to these letters. When they are published I shall add a volume of personal recollections of his later life; and this will be all. Had I been left unencumbered by special directions I should have been tempted to leave his domestic history untouched except on the outside, and have attempted to make a complete biography out of the general materials. This I am unable to do, and all that I can give the world will be materials for some other person to use hereafter. I can explain no further the conditions of the problem. But for my own share of it I have materials in abundance, and

I must avoid being tempted off into other matters however important in themselves.

'I may add for myself that I did not seek this duty, nor was it welcome to me. C. asked me to undertake it. When I looked through the papers I saw how difficult, how, in some aspects of it, painful, the task would be.

'Believe me,
'faithfully yours,
'J. A. FROUDE.'

[245a] Printed in 'Letters,' ii. 332.

[245b] July 30th.

[247] Printed in 'Letters,' ii. 333.

[248] Here begins second half-sheet, dated 'Monday, Sept. 5.'

[249] Partly printed in 'Letters,' ii. 335.

[250a] See letter of June 23rd, 1880.

[250b] Reprinted in 'A Book of Sibyls,' 1883.

[251a] *The Promise of May* was acted at the Globe Theatre, November 11th, 1882.

[251b] See letter of November 13th, 1879.

[252a] Mrs. Wister's son.

[252b] See letter of March 28th, 1880.

[253a] 'John Leech and other Papers,' 1882.

[253b] November 18th, 1882.

[257] See 'Letters and Memorials of Jane Welsh Carlyle,' ii. 249.

[259] For May 1883: 'Mrs. Carlyle.'

[260] Tennyson's 'Brook.'

[261] In a letter to Sir Frederick Pollock, March 16th, 1879, he says:—

"I have had Sir Walter read to me first of a Night, by way of Drama; then ten minutes for Refreshment, and then Dickens for Farce. Just finished the Pirate—as wearisome for Nornas, Minnas, Brendas, etc., as any of the Scotch Set; but when the Common People have to talk, the Pirates to quarrel and swear, then Author and Reader are at home; and at the end I 'fare' to like this one the best of the Series. The Sea scenery has much to do with this preference I dare say."

[263] See 'Letters,' ii. 344.

Lightning Source UK Ltd.
Milton Keynes UK
UKHW010716301222
414627UK00004B/292